W9-AUD-479

REBOOT!

WHAT TO DO WHEN YOUR CAREER
IS OVER BUT YOUR LIFE ISN'T

BY PHIL BURGESS

Published by:

FriesenPress
Suite 300 – 852 Fort Street
Victoria, BC, Canada V8W 1H8

www.friesenpress.com

Distributed to the trade by The Ingram Book Company

Excerpts from Reboot!

– on retirement

"Not all ideas are good ideas. Some are bad ideas. Retirement is one of those bad ideas – it makes no sense."

"Retirement is not natural. It is not historic. It is not healthy. It is not, for most people, fulfilling. For many, retirement is a widow maker."

"If retirement at age 65 were indexed to reflect increases in longevity since 1935, when Social Security was established, America's official retirement age would now be 82."

"If we must retire to something, we should not retire to retirement. We should retire to work. 'Work is made for man...'"

"Instead of retiring people, we should retire worn-out phrases like 'elders,' 'the elderly,' 'geriatrics,' 'geezers,' 'gummers,' 'gray beards,' 'the Golden Years' 'old fogey,' 'oldsters,' 'old-timer,' 'pensioners,' 'retirees.'"

"Many 'sixty somethings' are headed for the best years of their lives — including entrepreneurship, civic involvement, deeper friendships, heightened self-awareness, and increased wisdom and practical knowledge.   Some call 'the sixties' the new 'middle age.' Growing 'old' is not as grim as it used to be."

– on the value of work

"The social engagement and satisfaction that come from working in later life are key to successful aging."

"It is lifestyle – not wealth, race, or genetics – that plays the greatest role in allowing us to live well in later life. The lifestyle choices we make – including the decision to remain engaged through work – are keys to longevity and successful aging, not only in the US but in different cultures around the world."

"The luckiest among us will 'die with our boots on.' The reason is simple: The most healthy, productive, and satisfying transition to a post-career life will not be a transition from work-to-leisure but a transition from work-to-work – even though our post-career work may be very different from work we performed before we retired.

"There is much work to do in this world where we are but temporary inhabitants. We should find it and do it...at least for as long as we're able. In many ways, our life depends on it."

– on work and money

"Work is not only about money. Even if you don't need the money and your financial situation is stable and comfortable, returning to work in your post-career life is the smart thing to do – at least until sidelined by frailty or disability. It's smart because good health and satisfaction in later-life are most likely to come from working."

"Work is especially important when more than money matters."

"For some, later-life work is essential, especially if you didn't save enough or your 401k tanked in the Great Recession. In these cases, work will be tailored to meet the social, financial, and well-being needs you are likely to confront in your later years."

– on different types of work

"For most of us, post-career work will be tailored work, work customized to reflect our needs, our deepest desires, and the highest and best use of our gifts – especially time, talent, and treasure. Work tailored to our gifts will be productive and satisfying."

"Work comes in many flavors, especially in later-life when we have more flexibility. These include: (1) paid work, (2) in-kind work, (3) volunteer work, (4) Samaritan work, and (5) enrichment work. In each of these you have obligations and accountabilities to other people. That's always the case with every type of work."

"Because of the digital revolution, work in today's America can be performed in many locations: at home or the office, in the field or factory, or – with the rapid growth of the mobile Internet – on the go... e.g., from an RV, a marina, campground, or airport lounge."

What Others Are Saying About Reboot!

Why is *Reboot!* so great? Because people see themselves aging and wonder, "Is that all there is?" or "What do I do now?" Phil Burgess provides a surprising and uplifting answer to those questions – and it is not retirement. *Reboot!* is a must-read and perfect gift for anyone who even has a thought about "retiring" someday.

> – *John Mariotti, award-winning author of* The Complexity Crisis; *former President, Huffy Bicycles*

Phil Burgess rejects the idea of retirement into "Golden Years" of endless leisure and uses *Reboot!* to show why boomers will embrace work of some kind – such as paid work...or in-kind, volunteer, enrichment, or Samaritan work – to help others and make the world a better place.

> – *Barbara Nelson, Professor of Public Policy & Dean Emeritus, UCLA School of Public Affairs*

As retirement approached, a life of leisure looked less and less attractive. My friend Phil Burgess answered my prayers with *Reboot!* Intriguing, inspiring, and enjoyable to read, *Reboot!* gives real hope and shows why work in later life is good for the body and the spirit.

> – *Chaplain Norman F. Brown, U.S. Navy (ret.)*

America's boomers have redefined every stage of life in America, and they are now changing the aging game. *Reboot!* lays out the new rules. Rule #1: Keep working!

> – *Kent Briggs, Executive Director, Council of State Governments-West, Sacramento*

Phil Burgess has it exactly right. The last chapters of a life well lived should not be about retirement and decay; they should be about the joy of sharing your gifts, insights, and love with the generation that follows.

– Jeff Sandefer, Co-founder & Master Teacher, Acton School of Business, Austin, Texas

Reboot! has an important message for those thinking about their post-career years: What you want to be in your bonus years is much more important than what you want to do or what you want to have. Phil's book gave me new and helpful ways to approach this transition in my own life.

– Martin L. "Chip" Doordan, CEO, Anne Arundel Health System, Annapolis, Maryland

TABLE OF CONTENTS

Sidebars

Figures

RE·BOOT (REE-BOOT')
VERB (TRANS); NOUN

In computing

- Reboot means to restart or reset a computer. When a computer quits working, you push the reset button – that is, you turn it off, pause, and turn it back on. That allows the computer to reboot (or reload, reset, and restart) the systems that make it run. You also reboot when you buy new software applications to make the computer serve *your* needs and work for *your* purposes. When that happens, you load new software, such as desktop publishing, expense tracking, or games, and then reboot.

In filmmaking

- A reboot breathes fresh life into an old film, to attract new fans and stimulate new revenue. Film reboots sometimes recreate successful TV programs in a feature-length film format (such as *Hawaii Five-O, Rockford Files*), preserve franchises before they grow stale (such as *Planet of the Apes, Batman, or Spiderman)*, or revive old stories. Examples: *The Jazz Singer,* starring Al Jolson in 1927, was remade in 1953 with Danny Thomas and again in 1980 with Neil Diamond. In the 1999 reboot of *The Thomas Crown Affair,* Pierce Brosnan replaced Steve McQueen from the 1968 original. More recently, *True Grit*, a 2010 Coen brothers reboot starring Jeff Bridges, put a new spin on the 1969 original, directed by Henry Hathaway and starring John Wayne.

- In *television*, reboot means to modify some aspect of a TV program or series and start anew with fresh actors, ideas, themes, or sets. Familiar examples of pouring new wine into old bottles include *Sesame Street*, *Grey's Anatomy, Jeopardy,* and *Wheel of Fortune*.

And, don't forget footwear...

- In *footwear*, reboot means to refurbish shoes or boots so they can feel fresh and last longer, boosting longevity and durability by bringing them back to "footwear fitness" – a heel-to-toe makeover so they can continue to be used in a cleaner, brighter, or more functional state. Same old boots but with a new life and ready for new journeys. As Nancy Sinatra sang in her 1966 hit, "These boots were made for walkin', and that's just what they'll do..." Boots are not made to be stiffened by shoehorns and warehoused in a closet.

PREFACE

This book is about what to do when your career is over but your life isn't – what I call the post-career years. The typical answer to that question uses the verb *retire*, or refers to a condition called *retirement*.

My answer to that question is different, perhaps even blasphemy. My answer: **Go back to work.**

Work is not only about money. Even if you don't need the money, returning to work of some kind in your post-career life is the smart thing to do. It's smart because good health and satisfaction in later life are most likely to come from working. Work is essential if you didn't save enough for later life or your 401(k) tanked in the Great Recession. But work is also important when more than money matters.

The luckiest among us will die with our boots on. Even if our financial situation is stable and comfortable, we should look forward to working in some capacity until we are sidelined by frailty or disability. The reason is simple: The most healthy, productive, and satisfying transition to a post-career life will not be a transition from work to leisure but a transition from work to work – even though our post-career work may be very different from work we performed before we retired.

Preparing for post-career work means more of us will aim for a transition from career work performed during our working years to the tailored work we take up in our post-career life. By tailored work, I mean work customized to reflect our deepest desires and the highest and best use of our gifts of time, talent, and treasure. When we find work tailored to our gifts, we will be productive, and the work will be satisfying – and finding satisfaction in the work we do is important. Work should also be tailored to meet the social, financial, and lifestyle needs each of us is likely to confront in our later years. And for each of us, those needs will be different; hence, the kind of work we seek to do will be different – and will even vary during different stages of later life.

Work can and should be more than toil and drudgery; that is a core message of *Reboot!*. Work can and should be fulfilling and satisfying, especially when our work uses our gifts and reflects our purpose in life – what some writers call our calling. Work can also take many forms, particularly in later life when we have more flexibility.

In Chapter 8, we outline different work situations. Work can be full-time or part-time, for pay, or as a volunteer making a product or providing a service. You can do enrichment work to enhance your own personal growth and development. There is also what I call Samaritan work, which refers to person-to-person assistance or care-giving that growing numbers of later-life Americans are providing for parents or loved ones. Finally, because of the digital revolution, work in today's America can be performed in many locations: at home or the office, in the field or factory – or, with the rapid growth of the mobile Internet, on the go.

Reboot! **has five objectives**: (1) renovate the idea of work, (2) rethink the purpose of our post-career life, (3) redefine the idea and practice of retirement, (4) restructure the way we think about the passage or transition into the post-career chapters of our life, and (5) provide guidance and specific tips to the reader who is, or soon will be, making this transition to his or her post-career life – a transition, by the way, that affects women as much as men, especially for boomers, as increasing numbers of women have worked outside the home since the 1950s. In fact, in 2010 we reached a tipping point when, for the first time in modern history, there were more women than men in the workforce.

My own failed retirement, early in the first decade of the 21st century, is what prompted me to start looking into these issues of work, calling, and how we manage time – and particularly for what purpose – in our post-career life. I'm now several years into my second go – but I no longer call it retirement. Instead, I am now back to work, and things are going well. My experience with work in later life has been satisfying because I've practiced the ideas, strategies, and actions that I've discovered and outlined in the following pages. As Henry Ford said, "Failure is simply the opportunity to begin again, this time more intelligently."

Harry Moody, an official of the AARP,[2] wrote in a recent book review that "Gerontologists spend their lives studying aging but, with rare exceptions, have not much written about their personal experience of growing old."[3] I am not a gerontologist, nor in any formal way an expert in these matters, though early in my career I spent time on aging policy issues[4] and I am a participant-observer of my own aging and that of friends, neighbors, and colleagues. That means I'm probably more than a sandlot player but less than a major leaguer – perhaps more like a Little Leaguer or even a minor leaguer. But each of us, as we grow older, become self-educated experts, educated in the college of hard knocks where we learn from on-the-job experience of living, working, loving, succeeding, failing, and bouncing back. There are no degrees and no certificates of achievement. But there's lots of experience. It's that experience I share in the following pages – experience that is also informed by intensive study and rich and interesting conversations, both with experts and with peers who have struggled with the same issues of aging, work, leisure, and the search for meaning in later life.

I should also add that I have been fascinated by the experience of growing older. It is a lot more interesting than I thought it would be.

So here's the bottom line: **If we must retire to something, we should not retire to retirement**. We should retire to work. "Work is made for man..." as we shall see. There is much work to do in this world where we are but temporary inhabitants. We should find it, and we should do it – and that's how we should spend our post-career years...at least for as long as we're able. In many ways, our life depends on it.

CHAPTER 1
CHARTING A COURSE IN LATER LIFE

"Age is only a number, a cipher for the records. A man can't retire his experience. He must use it. Experience achieves more with less energy and time."
– Bernard Baruch

"I enjoy talking with very old people. They have gone before us on a road by which we, too, may have to travel, and I think we do well to learn from them what it is like."
– Socrates, in Plato's Republic

Time, a daily treasure that attracts many robbers.
– Anonymous

It's no accident you are holding this book. You've been hit by a discomforting reality: **Careers end way before life ends.** Put another way, people in later life are now retiring after 30 or 40 years of work – with most looking forward to 15 or 20 and maybe even 30 or more years of productive life.

You've picked up this book because you are already a later-life American[6] – or your partner, father, mother, a neighbor, or another loved one is. I am too.[7] The first wave of 78 million baby boomers – Americans born between 1946 and 1964 – began reaching retirement age in 2011. Indeed, there are now 41 million Americans 65 or older – a number that will nearly double over the next 18 years as boomers pass through age 65. Put another way, boomers are now retiring at the rate of 10,000 a day, and that will continue until 2030.[8]

Figure 1: Life-expectancy

Present Age	Years Left
50	+34.2
55	+29.6
60	+25.2
65	+21.0
70	+17.0
75	+13.4
80	+10.2
85	+ 7.6
90	+ 5.5
95	+ 4.1

Source: Internal Revenue Service (IRS). [5]

One result of this age wave[9] is a flood of books, retreats, magazines, workshops, and TV programs professing to help with the strategy of retirement, smart retirement, secure retirement, healthy retirement, meaningful retirement, enjoyable retirement, and the like. Most deal with:

- **wealth**, such as investments and financial management;
- **well-being**, such as nutrition, later-life fitness, and retirement living or long-term care;
- **lifestyle**, because the dominant cultural ideal is retirement to the good life during the Golden Years in a Sunbelt location; and, of course,
- **public policy**, such as the solvency of private pensions, Social Security, Medicare, and health care reform.[10]

Still, **too few touch on the most important later-life challenge**: What do you want *to be* and how can you live a life that matters in the bonus years – the extra years we will enjoy when our career is over, owing to increasing longevity. That's why this book is about the personal *you* and how you can think about the new world of later life that you and I and millions of other Americans are now negotiating.

The need to decide what you want to be came to me nearly 10 years ago during a luncheon conversation at the kitchen table with my wife, who painted a picture of how her life had changed since I retired – and it wasn't all for the better. She concluded by quoting the well-worn statement, "I married you for better or worse, but not for lunch." That's when I started to focus on what became the subtitle of this book: What to do when your career is over but your life isn't.

I talked to a lot of friends. I observed what other people were doing. I read a lot. I was especially educated by reading a study that has influenced more than a decade of research on the health and well-being of later-life Americans, a **study by the MacArthur Foundation that defined successful aging** as:

> "...the ability to maintain three key behaviors or characteristics: (1) low risk of disease and disease-related disability; (2) high mental and physical function; (3) active engagement with life...Active engagement with life takes many forms, but successful aging is most concerned with two – relationships with other people, and behavior that is productive ... It is this forward-looking, active engagement with life and with other human beings that is so critical to growing old well."[11]

Continued active engagement is the key. But that still leaves a lot of questions, like *how* to be engaged and for *what purposes*. That's when I came to conclusions that I share in this book.

To engage, you need a way to navigate. To navigate, you have to know your destination, and that is exactly what's missing for most of us in our post-career years. Here's the reason: As we move into our post-career years, we are transitioning from a highly scripted life of schedules, routines, obligations, and expectations to a largely unscripted life that will beg for structure, purpose, and meaning. This new life has been described as a "roleless" one, where it's no longer clear to people what is expected of them.[12]

If you are one of those people in the post-career phase of your life – or if you know one – then you know that deciding what to do in those unscripted years with lots of newfound time is a daunting challenge. For the first time in a long time – perhaps since you graduated from high school or college, embarked on your first job, or decided to get married and have a family – you are faced with rethinking how best to use your major gifts:

- how to manage your **time,**
- how to apply your **talent** and use your skills, and
- how to use your **treasure** – and not just money, but also other assets, such as your knowledge, wisdom, experience,

and temperament.

But there is guidance. In addition to the MacArthur study, others, focused on US populations, come to a similar conclusion – namely that **lifestyle choices play the greatest role in allowing people to live well in later life** – not wealth, race, or genetics.[13] A recent multi-national, multicultural study entitled *The Blue Zone* also found our lifestyle and the choices we make are the keys to longevity across different cultures around the world.[14]

So, like every other chapter of life, **later life is about choices.** Later life is about deciding how to live and what to do with your gifts of time, talent, and treasure – including the knowledge, skills, experience, wisdom, and resources gained over many years – as you begin each day of what should be the most creative and rewarding period of your life.[15]

The realities of increasing longevity and the improved health enjoyed by most later-life Americans require us to revise our thinking and the language we use to talk about later life – and specifically the post-career years. The realities of growing older are changing, so the words we use must also change.[16]

Instead of retiring people, we should retire worn-out words like elders, the elderly, geriatrics, geezers, gummers, gray beards, old fogies, oldsters, old-timers, pensioners, retirees – and worn-out phrases like the Golden Years.[17] The reason is increasing longevity, arguably the greatest achievement of the 20th century – when life expectancy soared more than two-thirds from 47 years in 1900 to 77 years in 2000.[18] These old labels have passed their use-by date and should be poured down the drain like curdled milk. [19]

Other old ideas about later life also need to be jettisoned – beginning with the idea that aging is primarily about pathologies. Sure, bad things do happen as we grow older, and the downsides to growing longer in the tooth are well known, well documented, and discussed *ad nauseam* – including loss of social identity, financial insecurity, and fading physical and sometimes mental well-being.

As one of my friends said on his way to physical therapy several weeks after a successful quadruple by-pass, "Growing old ain't easy", echoing Bette Davis' assertion that "Growing old ain't for sissies."

My first personal experience with fading well-being came a few years ago when my orthopedic surgeon (a no-nonsense, plain-spoken physician) set me straight, as I tried to give him a way to put a happy face on my pending knee replacement surgery. I asked, "So, it sounds like you think my knees will be better after this operation?" He replied, pointing down to the frayed edge of his office carpet, "If we glue down this carpet, will the carpet get better? No!

Of course not! It just won't wear out as fast. It's the same with your knees. At your age, our challenge is to retard the rate of deterioration. Nothing will, as you say, get better."

While that grim verdict might not be literally true – because there are many things we can do to improve our later-life health and performance[20] – my physician's verdict that we will inevitably slow down and experience physical and mental deterioration is generally true. Indeed, as Lord Keynes famously said, "In the long run we are all dead!"

Until that fateful day comes, however, **it is important to appreciate the many upsides to aging and benefits of growing maturity.**[21] These benefits and advantages are under-rated and should be recognized and understood as we begin to reshape how we think about our own later-life years. Indeed, later life is a time when a lot of good things happen, including:

- **increased practical knowledge** of life,
- **expanded understanding** of people, places, and the way things work,
- **increased wisdom** that comes from combining knowledge with experience,
- **more tried-and-tested skills** and a better feel for your abilities and limits,
- **heightened self-awareness,**
- **deeper relationships,** and more appreciation of their importance,
- **increased spirituality,** compared to younger ages, and
- **more textured understanding of the meaning of life, suffering, and death**.

Being 50, 60, 70, or even 80 is different from the old days. Growing old is not as grim as it used to be.[22]

- **Nearly all fifty-somethings are more adventurous** and leading more active and engaged lifestyles – and the new energy of later-life Americans often continues into their seventies, eighties, and nineties.[23]

- **Most sixty-somethings are headed for the best years of their lives** – including more entrepreneurship, increased political activism, closer friendships, and continued good sex.[24] Some call the sixties "the new middle age."
- **Many in their seventies and some in their eighties and nineties** remain actively engaged in business, politics, family, and community service – including part-time or full-time volunteer work and some in paid jobs, part-time or even full-time.

Given the blessing of good health and longevity that most of us will enjoy in our post-career years, the challenge we face is to find a way to script the remaining years of our life so our post-career years will be purposeful, productive, and satisfying – and perhaps even rewarding and consequential.

I learned of the need for a script and the value of work the hard way. I failed in my first retirement at age 60 because I failed to take a time-out to chart a course or write a script for my post-career years. Like many others I've come to know, I simply glided into my post-career life on auto-pilot. Looking back, maybe I should say drifted or stumbled. Whatever word is used, my transition to post-career life was not mindful.[25]

When people asked what I planned to do with my free time and how I would use my newfound freedom, I gave the auto-pilot answer: "I'll catch up on my reading, sign up for piano lessons, spend more time on the water, travel with the family, and take it easy for a while." I once included "brush up on my tennis game," but that came off the list when I got the two new knees mentioned earlier. Still, like many others, I looked forward to a period of relaxation, enjoyment, and enrichment. After all, that's what I had worked for all these years. It was now time to reap the benefits, hang up the spurs, and cash in. So I did.

Healthy Aging

*"Successful aging, like sobriety and feeling tickled,
can best be achieved in a relationship."*
– George Vaillant

George Vaillant, M.D., is the author of *Aging Well: Surprising Guideposts to a Happier Life*, a groundbreaking book on adult human development based on findings from Harvard's landmark Study of Adult Development, which he directed. In the words of the summary, Vaillant's "surprising conclusion is that individual lifestyle choices play a greater role than genetics, wealth, race, or other factors in determining how happy people are in later life." Factors assessed before age 50 that predict healthy aging, and those that do not, are shown below.[291] Additional factors from an assessment study of successful aging research are *shown in italics*.[292]

Factors that *do* predict healthy aging	Factors that *do not* predict healthy aging
1. Nonsmoker, or stopping young	1. Ancestral longevity
2. Adaptive coping style, mature defenses[293]	2. Cholesterol
	3. Stress
3. Absence of alcohol use	4. Parental characteristics
4. Healthy weight	5. Childhood temperament
5. Stable marriage	6. General ease in social relationships
6. Some exercise	
7. *Higher activity levels*	7. *Gender*
8. *Years of education*	8. *Income*
9. *Social activities*	
10. *Productive activities*	
11. *Contact with friends*	

During the first six months or so, my wife and I spent more time with our kids and more time on our boat.[26] We read a lot more. We took in more movies. We visited friends and relatives in other states. We worked around the house and spruced up the landscape. We got more involved in our local community and in the many cultural events that thrive in the larger metro areas of Washington, D.C. and Baltimore that surround the historic town of Annapolis where we live. As my new post-career life unfolded, I even got too busy for piano lessons.

POST-CAREER YEARS: A SCORECARD

Direction -> Effect	Positive	Negative
Personal	Heightened self-awareness Increased: • experience • knowledge • skills • understanding • wisdom Greater understanding of the meaning of: • life • suffering • death More time for reflection	Declining health Chronic infirmities Multiple medical problems Increasing disability: • physical: e.g., frailty • psychological: e.g., depression • mental: e.g., memory loss, senility Slowing down of everything Reduced income
Social	More patient, more accepting of other people, less aggressive Increased appreciation of the needs of others Increased time for: • part-time or full-time work • community service, volunteer activities, and giving back • family, care-giving • enrichment work: fitness, hobbies, study, travel • leisure, recreation	Less tolerant of certain behavior, ideas Loss of: • status • authority • power • visibility • external validation • standing

But taking it easy got old...quickly. I was hit by boredom and a sense of emptiness, reminding me of Peggy Lee's old song, "Is that all there is?" About that time, a friend told me he was going down to the Center for Creative Leadership in Greensboro, North Carolina, an institution I have long respected but had never visited.

I decided to ride along. When we arrived, I discovered that author and change management expert Bill Bridges, a man whose books and articles I had read and respected, was leading a two-day workshop on transitions. So, I decided to stay over to attend. That's when I learned all transitions need to include a formal time-out to reflect on the past and develop a plan for the future. [27]

Once I returned home, that's what I did. I set aside time each day to give attention to my own future. I became more mindful about my own situation. I did a lot of reading. I visited with people I know who had been through or who were going through the same post-career experience. I thought a lot about what I had done and what I would do to manage my time in wise, productive, and satisfying ways during the next few years.

It was during my long-neglected time-out that I came to understand my strong need to do something consequential, something that would make a difference, and something that would help give meaning to the newfound gift of time I was experiencing. I also had an urge to continue to develop and use the knowledge and skills I had acquired over years of living, learning, and doing in my career days. In fact, I really wanted to go back to work in some capacity, where I could be useful, make a contribution, and help do work that needed to be done.

I came out of my time-out with a new script for my post-career life. When people asked me about my plans for later life, I could now say, with some confidence, "I want to be a teacher. That's what I have always been. That's what I want to be going forward. I want to do activities related to teaching – leading, advising, mentoring, advocating, speaking, and writing. What I want to have is a result that is some combination of fun, lucrative, and consequential." Let me repeat that:

- fun,
- lucrative, and
- consequential.

By fun, I meant doing something enjoyable, something for which I could happily set the alarm clock each night and look forward to doing the next day after a swim and a good breakfast.

By lucrative, I meant doing something that has personal benefit or pay-off. The benefit could be money, but it could also be peace of mind or the satisfaction of a job well done.

By consequential, I meant doing something that would have positive results that could make a difference for my family, friends, neighbors, or the larger community; leave a legacy or give something back; or perhaps advance a cause or support a movement. A cause could include everything from feeding the hungry, helping a local nonprofit, or campaigning for (or against) a political reform, to going back to work in a job that contributes to the productivity of an enterprise or provides products or services to others.

I was confident that I had thoughtfully re-scripted my life around being a teacher. My objectives were fun, lucrative, and consequential. I wanted to get back to work in some capacity where I could apply my skills and work with others toward shared objectives.

About that time, and totally out of the blue, I got a call from a close friend and former colleague. It was a Thursday night in late June 2005. After some small talk, he asked, "How would you like to go back to work?"

"Tell me more," I replied.

His response: "I am going to Sydney to lead Australia's largest telecommunications company. Why don't you come along and help me with the transition and maybe stay for a while?" [28]

Here was an offer to come off the bench and get back onto the playing field. My decision took a nanosecond. I said, "Yes, where do I go, and when should I get there?"

He said, "Can you be in Sydney next week, like on Monday?"

"See you then," I replied.

With three days of preparation, which included finding my passport and securing the blessing of my wife, [29] I took off for Sydney, Australia, arriving on July 5, 2005. I lived in the great Down Under for more than three years – until October 2008. It was during that experience of getting back on the clock that much of this book took shape – as my wife and I lived out a new way to think about retirement. [30]

CHAPTER 2

THE ONSET OF LATER LIFE

"Grow old along with me! The best is yet to be, the last of life,
for which the first was made".
– Robert Browning

"Forty is the old age of youth; fifty is the youth of old age."
– Victor Hugo

"So teach us to number our days, that we may apply our
hearts unto wisdom"
– Psalm 90[12]

"The years between fifty and seventy are the hardest. You are always asked
to do things, and you are not yet decrepit enough to turn them down."
– TS Eliot

"When men reach their sixties and retire, they go to pieces.
Women go right on cooking."
– Gail Sheehy

When does later life begin? It began for me when I turned 50. And whether you know it or not, age 50 is when it will happen to you, too. It's not a physical or psychological thing; it's a cultural thing.

It happened to me when I came home one day to find that the US Postal Service had delivered a letter, personally addressed to me, from the American Association of Retired Persons – now known simply as AARP.[31] The package included a letter, a membership form, and the current copy of *Modern Maturity*, the AARP magazine.[32]

I must say, however, that receiving correspondence from the AARP at the age of 50, having just finished a decade of telling people, "I'm in my forties", was like receiving a letter from the Centers for Disease Control marked CONFIDENTIAL. I was shocked. Now the mail carrier knows. Who else knows? The magazine looks interesting, but where can I hide it so guests won't see it? I wondered if anyone noticed the AARP magazine in my mail box. Why is this all happening now, I thought? Doesn't retirement begin at 65?

It turns out there were lots of other people keeping tabs on me. During the next few months, I received many other letters – letters to get a bowel screening, letters to get a PSA test for prostate cancer, letters to get a vascular screening. I discovered there are all kinds of people out there who not only knew me but who were really concerned about my health since I had turned 50. What would it be like to reach age 65?

GEORGE CARLIN ON AGING[294]

Comedian George Carlin famously observed that "...the only time in our lives when we like to get old is when we're kids, [noting that] if you're less than 10 years old, you're so excited about aging that you think in fractions.

"How old are you? 'I'm four *and a half!*' You're never thirty-six *and a half.* You're four *and a half*, going on five! That's the key."

He then notes that you become 21, turn 30, push 40, reach 50, make it to 60, hit 70, get to your eighties...but "if you make it over one hundred, you become a little kid again. 'I'm a hundred-and-a-half.'"

Actually, in my experience, many return to fractions in their nineties. And good for them! In the meantime, as George Carlin said, "May you all make it to a healthy one hundred...*and a half*!"

Actually, there is nothing at all special about age 65, and there is certainly no reason to retire at 65. The idea of retiring at age 65 was introduced to the public dialogue by Prussian Chancellor Otto von Bismarck, the general and head of government, who in 1883 proposed and in 1888 established the world's first social security system.[33]

Bismarck was a smart general who defeated France in the Franco-Prussian war of 1870-71, starting a trend of Germans whipping the French whenever a war came up. Bismarck was an even smarter politician. At least he could count, unlike many of today's politicians. Bismarck was smart because he set the retirement age at 65 when the life expectancy for Germans was less than 45. Because the average Tom, Dick and Heinrich didn't live to see 45, this Prussian social policy innovation had a nice spin but did not deplete the nation's treasury, nor touch the lives of most people. At the turn of the 20th century, life expectancy had risen to 47, still no threat to the budget of a government obligated to fund retirement at age 65.[34]

One-third of the way into the next century, barking up the same tree, US President Franklin D. Roosevelt established America's own Social Security program. Like Bismarck 50 years earlier, FDR also set the retirement age at 65 years. However, that was 1935 and things had changed since 1888. Life expectancy for the average American had climbed from 47 years at the turn of the century to 62 years in 1935. Fast forward to today: The Social Security retirement age is *still* age 65 (recently advanced to 67 for those born in 1960 or later), but overall life expectancy has now climbed to 78 years and it is still increasing. If we were to perform an "FDR longevity adjustment" to US Social Security, **today's official retirement age would be 82 years – not 65 years.**[35]

If Americans had to wait until age 82 to get their Social Security check, one thing's for certain: We would not have the financial crisis in the Social Security trust fund we are now facing. It is interesting to note the same elected leaders who are quick to index cost-of-living to their salaries will not index the retirement age.

The real problem today is that American culture continues to crave longevity at the same time it idealizes retirement – and retirement at earlier and earlier ages. Consider the following cover stories and headlines from some of our most widely read newspapers and magazines:

- "Your Dream Retirement: How to Make It Happen" – *Reader's Digest* (October 2001)
- "The Rise of the Alpha Geezer" – *Washington Post* (September 9, 2007)
- "How to Live to be 100" – *USN&WR* (February 2010)

Even worse, books abound encouraging us to "retire early and live well."[36] In fact, retirement age declined from age 67 in the early 1950s through the 1990s, when it hit age 60. However, **the average age is now 62 as both men and women delay retirement** – with more than 50 percent reporting they do it as a way to earn more money, retain health benefits, and stay active. [37]

Most disturbing is the view that retiring early is considered a virtue. A twenty-something stockbroker whom I see now and then at the pool where I swim told me one day his driving ambition is to retire when he is 45. "To do what?" I asked. He looked at me like I was from another planet and repeated, slowly, "To...re...tire!" I think it was only good manners that kept him from responding, "To retire, stupid!"

THE SOCIAL SECURITY TIME BOMB

Until 2010, the Social Security fund was cash-flow positive – meaning it was taking in more money that it was paying out. In 2010 that changed when the Social Security fund turned cash-flow negative, earlier than expected owing to the Great Recession. Cash-flow negative means Social Security is paying out more to recipients (retirees) than it is receiving in cash from working people paying in.

This is the Social Security crisis that so many talk about. America's Social Security system is a pay-as-you-go system. It is not based on savings placed in a lockbox or invested; rather Social Security is a simple transfer from the payroll taxes that people now working pay into the government to cover the Social Security checks that same government delivers to retirees.

In 1950, there were 16 people working – paying Social Security taxes into the government – for each retiree getting a benefit check. Today, that number is three workers paying in for each person receiving a check, and this will decrease to two workers per beneficiary by the time all the baby boomers have retired.

Bottom line: The Social Security formula doesn't compute. Something has to give: higher payroll taxes, later retirement age, needs-testing, reduced benefits, or some combination. The status quo cannot be sustained. Put another way, promises made will not be kept. You can bank on that!

Some of us will truly retire between ages 50 and 65, maybe earlier, maybe later. Many of us will never retire; instead, we will die with our boots on. But nearly all of us, at some age, will leave our career behind as we begin to explore our post-career life.

In a practical sense, **the challenging part of later life begins when you leave your career or your regular work.** That may be age 50 – or even earlier during an economic downturn – but it will more likely be much later, like 60, 62, or 65. For some, especially so-called knowledge workers who provide business and professional services or advanced manufacturing, it may reach into the late sixties or early seventies.[38] That post-career phase of your life begins when you decide to hang up your spurs. That decision often is affected by one or more considerations, some controllable, some not:

- **Personal preference or need**: You may go for early retirement to be free of the obligations of a job you no longer enjoy. On the other hand, you may have financial needs that can only be met by continuing to work as long as possible.

- **Personal health**: Bad knees and bad backs often lead to the early retirement of electricians, painters, carpenters, surgeons, and dentists, for example. Good health, on the other hand, often leads to a desire to extend your established working career.

- **Financial well-being of your employer**: If he's in trouble, your leaving early may help. If he's expanding, you may be given financial or other incentives to delay your retirement, such as flex work, longer vacations, shorter work days, or shorter work weeks.

- **Health of the economy**: A weak economy may lead to a pink slip-induced retirement. A boom may lead to a bonus if you remain on the job.

- **Laws or regulations** of a state, public agency, or the by-laws of a corporation that include mandatory retirement – the requirement for people to end their employment at a certain age, sometimes as early as 50 or 60 (especially airline pilots, firefighters, police, career military), or more typically at 65 or even 70.[39]

Bottom line: There is seldom a right time to step aside and enter the post-career phase of your life. Timing for retirement varies widely for all kinds of reasons unique to each individual and to the environment in which he or she is working.

Still, to frame our discussion, it helps to put a number to when later life begins. For convenience, let's stipulate later life begins at 50 and ends when life ends. Fifty is the age many later-life institutions, like AARP and insurance companies, use to identify their constituency. Age 50 is also when many health concerns begin for men (e.g., prostate cancer) and women (e.g., breast cancer), although these maladies can strike at any age. Age 50 is also a milestone picked by many who aspire to so-called early retirement.

So, for our purposes here, we'll accept what many others assert: Later life begins at 50. Yet it is sometime after 50 when most of us will enter the post-career phase of later life – and this book is about the post-career years and how we use them. For a few of us, the post-career years will begin before 60. For most of us, those years will begin after 60, and for some, many years after 60. [40]

CHAPTER 3
THE COMFORT OF A SCRIPTED LIFE

"Alice came to a place where there were many roads. She stopped and asked the owl for directions. The owl responded, 'Do you know where you want to go?' Alice said, 'No.' 'Well then,' the owl said, 'it doesn't make any difference which path you take.'"
– Lewis Carroll, Alice in Wonderland

Think about it. Almost all your life is scripted.

From the earliest days of infancy to that memorable first day of school, your life is scripted by your parents, perhaps with some scribbling in the margins by sisters and brothers or perhaps grandparents or an aunt or uncle.

From kindergarten through high school or university, whenever you terminate your formal education, your life is scripted by teachers, coaches, the requirements of school, and increasingly peers (your friends and the crowd you hang with, especially during the teenage years), as well as the media.[41]

Then you get married and enter the job market. For the next 30 to 40 years, your life is scripted by your partner and by your boss, or in the words of comedy writer Gene Perret, "When you retire, you switch bosses – from the one who hired you to the one who married you."

In short, **your life is scripted by your family and your culture** – including the culture of the enterprise where you work, the community and neighborhood where you live, and the daily give and take, honey-do lists, and nurturing and chauffeuring of children that shape the rhythms of family life.

If you are a stay-at-home mom (or dad, which happens more often these days), your life is scripted by the demands of homemaking and the academic calendar and extra-curricular schedules of children - hockey training and soccer tryouts, plus swimming practices, speech contests, and scout meetings. As we move through life, we are never at a loss for someone to tell us what to do and when to do it. Our life is structured from the morning alarm until lights out by obligations and schedules...and that goes for the kids too. By the time they are teenagers they'll have a schedule to keep - and chances are they'll have a Nokia or perhaps even an iPhone or BlackBerry to prove it.

Somewhere along the way, the kids leave home to go on to college or university, take a job, or get married. For most parents that happens somewhere between 40 and 50 years old. At that point we become empty nesters - kids gone, a new life beckons, and for the first time, scripting your life becomes more flexible, more open-ended, providing more choices, and more degrees of freedom.

With an empty nest, there is usually more opportunity to:
- improvise,
- change the routine,
- make up for lost time,
- try your wings in new environments,
- have more time to yourself, and
- exercise more freedom and have more freedom to exercise.

But often there are detours and unexpected journeys, such as aging parents to take care of or kids who are still around (or have moved back in between jobs, after lost jobs, or a failed marriage).[42] Indeed, many of us fall into the sandwich generation, one that takes care of aging parents even as our own kids still live at home.

Even with empty nesters, there is often someone in the family who is still in the workplace - so he or she is still scripted by a daily schedule that is largely written by someone else, such as a boss or customers or bankers. Because one partner is still engaged in the workplace, the other will often go back to work just to keep busy or to find a way to be useful to a business or a cause or simply to earn some extra money to build up the retirement fund, pay the kids' tuition, or fund a long-awaited vacation. Result: Empty nest years often remain scripted and, for some, become even more scripted than before - intended or not.

Bottom line: Most of our life is scripted - by parents, family, peers, schools, faith institutions, neighborhood, community, or workplace

– and for some of us by the boss from hell.[43] Whatever our situation, we go through most of our life with a pretty clear idea of what we are expected to do, and most of us do it, whether we like it or not.

CHAPTER 4
ENTERING THE
UNSCRIPTED LIFE

*"The only choice that can't be justified is
retiring to a life of do-nothingness."*
– Marie Beynon Ray [44]

*"I arise in the morning, torn between a desire to improve the world and a
desire to enjoy the world. It makes it hard to plan the day."*
– E.B. White [45]

Somewhere between 50 and 65 years, most working Americans typically leave their job and finish off their career – with the average person leaving at age 62.[46] They quit work. The house is paid for. The kids are educated. The career is over. But life goes on – and in some cases, especially in these days of medical miracles – on and on and on.[47]

Enter what can be the long night of post-career longevity and the shock of the unscripted life.

Some get a gold watch and a big send-off. At least we used to. These days, more of us simply pack up, say our farewells, and head for the highly anticipated good life. Then we wake up the next day or the next week to find a new and unsettling reality that can be disorienting, with:

- no agenda,
- no obligations,
- no accountabilities,
- no schedule to keep,
- no one telling us what to do,
- no expectations that have to be met,

- no rules or regulations, beyond those imposed by the state and your mate.

Put another way, to retire is to experience an abrupt transition from a highly scripted life of schedules, routines, expectations, obligations, and accountabilities, to a largely unscripted life where, to paraphrase the tune made famous by the Mamas and the Papas, "You can go where you wanna go. / Do what you wanna do."[48]

Glossy ads tell you these are the Golden Years. Cover stories on *Outdoor* magazine encourage you to take that long-postponed trek. *Golf Digest, Tennis View,* and *Cruising Magazine* scream out that you should try more golfing, tennis, or coastal sailing when you are 45 or 50 or 55 – why wait till 65?

Money magazine – and *Worth* and the *Kiplinger Letter* – will tell you how to manage your money so it will last as long as you do. Later-life celebrities, like film star Robert Wagner and former US Senator and film star Fred Thompson, will tell you how to get a reverse mortgage to fund the Golden Years for those short of money because they didn't save enough during their wage-earning years, or their 401(k) tanked in the stock market meltdown. G. Gordon Liddy of Watergate fame will implore you to invest in gold: "It never goes down," he assures inquiring minds and undecided prospects.

And it doesn't stop with money management. *Fitness* magazine will tell you how you can live better and last longer if you devote just 60 minutes a day to sweat-producing exercise. They launder the process by calling it pilates or aerobic exercise. That makes it sound less demanding, more scientific, and hopefully more palatable. And the new Retirement Living TV channel – called RLTV – packages much of this financial and lifestyle advice and presents it on cable TV in a more easily digestible, even entertaining, format.

There is also a pitch to *lone eagles* – people seeking a new life by moving to a new location after they retire. Still, the fact is fewer than five percent of us move to America's celebrated retirement meccas - e.g., the American Southwest, the west coast of Florida, the Ozarks, the barrier islands of the Carolinas, or any other of America's mild and wild areas. Moreover, some of those who make the move quickly tire of the good life in a new location and after a few years return to the old hometown.[49] I call these people *homing pigeons* – post-career Americans who find paradise to be less than they expected.[50]

The fact is that most of us stay home in the first place. Home is familiar. Home is where we have friends, neighbors, and social networks. Home is where we have ties to our butcher, baker, broker, and banker – as well as our physician, pharmacist, plumber, and pastor. We are reassured by the tailgate tribe at football games and faith-based fellowships that meet on the Sabbath and sometimes during the week. We value the service clubs like Rotary and Kiwanis that assemble like-minded people committed to community service and civic improvement. And, if our kids live in the area, we often are attracted by the most powerful magnet of all – grandkids.[51] As American humorist and writer Sam Levenson said, "The reason grandchildren and grandparents get along so well is because they have a common enemy."

Still, magazines from *Fortune* and *Forbes* to *People, Money,* and *Newsweek* will tell you where later-life Americans are moving and which retirement communities are best suited to your lifestyle preferences, your health and well-being, and your pocketbook. Never mind that most people stay put.[52]

So, when you look around, you find all kinds of help about where to live,[53] what to eat, how to stay fit, and how to invest your money and manage what's left. However, there is precious little on how you should manage your time – as opposed to spend your time. You can spend your time watching TV, gardening, golfing, playing cards, going to the club, or sitting on the bench in the town square, but that is not managing your time.

Of all the pitches to those in later life, the fitness pitch is perhaps the most relevant to successful aging. Research clearly shows there are multiple physical and mental benefits to regular exercise.[54] Indeed, one reason age 60-plus is called the new middle age is because later-life Americans are paying more attention to fitness. And for good reason: I remember attending a lecture in Dallas by Cooper Clinic founder, Dr. Kenneth Cooper, the former Air Force physician who invented what we call aerobics.[55] He said, "When all is said and done, people should seek fitness because fit people live longer, live better and die faster." Put simply, fit people, more often than the unfit, dodge the bullet of the lingering death.[56]

There are, unfortunately, very few pitches to the most important question of all – and that is how you should manage your time, a gift you have in abundance after you retire. **Managing your time implies a purpose. You always manage to a purpose.** So the real question to ask and answer is what should we do, and why should we do it? To what end should we spend our time, and how is that decision enabled or blocked by our treasure?

LATER-LIFE MIGRATION

Contrary to popular opinion, most later-life Americans do not move. They stay put.

- Migration is heavily concentrated in young adulthood.
- 14 in 100 Americans aged 10 move in a typical year,
- 34 in 100 aged 20 are movers, compared with
- 16 in 100 aged 30, and just
- 8 in 100 aged 50.
- Mobility rates are also slightly higher for men than for women.[295]

However, migration in later life is still important, for at least two reasons.

First, those who do migrate tend to be the more affluent Americans in the middle to upper income categories. So their impact on the civic and economic life of a destination can be significant.

Second, because the number of people in the 65-plus category is increasing dramatically, the absolute number of later-life Americans on the move will increase substantially even if the percentage of movers may stay the same.

Here you are, at the top of your game – gifted in many ways, full of wisdom born of knowledge tempered by experience. You are in generally good health, despite a few aches and pains and a longer recovery time when something does go wrong. You are still able to make a contribution to society – to the life of a community or the well-being of a child, an extended family member, or a friend. But there is a set of problems:

- you have no menu of options,
- you have no roadmap to guide your post-career journey, and
- you have no platform or base of operations.

In short, you have no script and no stage. To make matters worse, you are not skilled in writing a script; you are experienced in following a script. And there is very little to alert you to the need or to help you assemble a script for the rest of your life.

TIME: USE IT OR LOSE IT

Imagine a bank that credits your account each morning with $86,400. Then every evening it deletes whatever part of the balance you failed to spend or invest during the previous day. What would you do? Spend all of it, every day, of course!

Each of us has such a bank. Its name is time. Every morning, it credits you with 86,400 seconds. Every night it writes off, as lost forever, whatever of this you failed to spend or invest to good purpose during the day. It carries over no balance. It allows no overdraft.

Each day it opens a new account for you. Each night it confiscates what remains unspent from the day. If you fail to use the day's deposit, the loss is yours and can't be recovered.

There are no savings you can go back to, and you can't get an advance or otherwise draw on tomorrow. You must live in the present, on today's deposit. Spend and invest your time – 86,400 seconds each day – so as to get from it the utmost in health, happiness, and whatever else brings meaning to your life. The clock is running. Make the most of today.[296]

That's what this book is about: It is about scripting the unscripted life. It is about:

- how you should think about the opportunities and options of your post-career years,
- what you should do with your gifts of time, talent, and treasure, and
- how you can use your post-career years to finish well, living a life that matters.

It doesn't matter where you live. It doesn't matter whether you have a fully stuffed 401(k), a depleted 401(k), or income that depends exclusively on a monthly check from Social Security – though your financial condition obviously will influence what you are able to do and the options you have. At the same time, you can change your financial condition by making good choices. In fact,

Fortune magazine published a special issue with a cover story that screams, "You can still retire rich."[57]

The bottom line is this: Whatever the reality of your financial resources and your living situation or location, you cannot escape the requirement to decide what to do with your time – your most important non-renewable resource. Your talents can be polished or learned anew. Your treasure can grow, be depleted, or be replaced. But time, once used, is gone forever.

MANAGING TO A PURPOSE

Managing your time is different from managing your other assets. When you manage your **money**, there are objective markers and widely accepted benchmarks for evaluating your decisions, such as return on investment or solvency. When you manage your **health**, there are clear external markers, such as fitness. When you manage your **nutrition**, there are clear external markers of healthy eating. But when you manage your **time**, the markers depend on internal factors based on your values and your worldview. Moreover, time is different from every other resource, because time, once spent, cannot be replaced. That's why the decisions we make about how we use time in our post-career life require us to be clear about how we think about our life's purpose and how we live a life of meaning – an issue we address in Chapter 13.

That's why you need to write a script for the rest of your life. Though every message from society (media, family, financial advisor, pastor) is telling you to take it easy, to disengage, to retire to live the good life, the fact is social engagement is the surest path to successful aging.[58] The challenge: Find a way to engage with other people around projects or activities where you are accountable to someone for your performance and where you participate in the events of your family, community and country. [59]

CHAPTER 5
PITFALLS OF THE UNSCRIPTED LIFE

"Nobody grows old merely by living a number of years.
We grow old from a lack of purpose. Years may wrinkle the skin. Lack
of purpose wrinkles the soul."
-Samuel Ullman[60]

When I retired at age 60, I was happy as a clam. Now I could do all the things I wanted to do. I could read more books. I would now have the time to reflect on and rekindle old relationships, and re-visit old dreams. My wife and I could go sailing on the Chesapeake Bay or down the Intracoastal Waterway to Florida. We could get in the car and visit our kids, who were attending universities in nearby states. Because I would have less out-of-town travel, I could more regularly attend my local Rotary Club in Annapolis and get more involved in community service. Retirement seemed like everything I had ever wanted.

It didn't work out that way. All of a sudden my phone didn't ring so much. My email traffic thinned out dramatically. I quickly came face-to-face with an unpleasant reality – a reality, I've learned, that many others experience at the end of their career, namely the growing realization that many relationships we value on a personal level are in fact primarily work (or role) related. When I left my position by retiring, many of my relationships continued, but too many dissolved, some abruptly. This was sometimes a disappointment, but it is understandable. Truth be told, we are often lured (I should say, we lure ourselves) into thinking we are valued because of who we are as individuals and what we know and what we can do – and not the position we hold or the role we play in a team or an organization.

Another reality: Much of my personal identity and sense of self-worth were bundled with what I did in my work. Much of the joy in my life came from working with others – creating, innovating, solving problems, mentoring, and helping to make things happen. Indeed, I discovered shortly after I retired that I needed to work – that is, I needed to be engaged in some kind of productive activity where I could use my gifts and remain true to my calling. To paraphrase Descartes: "I work; therefore I am." But I failed to ask, "I am what?" or "Work to what end, to what purpose?"

WORK AND IDENTITY

In discussing how work is related to human dignity, Harvard political theorist, Russell Muirhead writes, "Along with family and religion, work remains one of the central activities constituting everyday life. Work is instrumental (we work to earn and spend), but is rarely only that: it is also formative. Devoting the bulk of our waking hours to a particular activity over many years has an effect on who we are, whether we like it or not. In a limited but crucial way, we are what we do ('What do you do?' is a kind of shorthand for 'Who are you?')...What we do habituates and orients us in profound ways that over time impress a pattern on our emotional and intellectual life. Work might make us more compassionate or more stern, more decisive or more resentful, more deft or more argumentative...This is why work for many cannot be merely another of life's routines, but is rather a key source of their identity."[297]

In their book on *Wellbeing*, Tom Rath and Jim Harter discuss how our careers shape not only our identity but also our wellbeing, noting a study that shows how we recover from major life events, such as separation from work, marriage, divorce, birth of a child, or death of a spouse.[298] The study shows that even though people do recover to the same level of wellbeing following most events, even the death of a spouse, the recovery period for separation from work is much more prolonged: "Our wellbeing actually recovers more rapidly from the death of a spouse than it does from a sustained period of unemployment."[299] Again, our role as a worker shows up as a major element of our being, not just our doing.

Therefore, early in my post-career life – before I learned of the need to take a time-out to think things through and to decide what I wanted to be in my post-career life – I looked for things to do, I'm sure to resurrect a sense of purpose in my life.

- When the head of a local school called for advice about fundraising, I not only gave it, but volunteered to help organize a fundraising advisory group.
- When a technology magazine invited me to give a series of speeches in far-off places about the impact of the digital revolution on society, I said yes.
- When a friend asked me to help him get a new nonprofit organization off the ground, I did it.
- When a family asked me to help them set up a family foundation, I said OK, and devoted several rewarding months to that exercise.
- When a friend of a friend asked me to advise him on how to generate revenues to preserve a stunning historic property in Washington, D.C., I agreed, and we did it.

Some of these things I did pro bono, for free. Some generated fees, which put money in the bank to let me buy toys, pay for entertainment, subsidize college tuition for my kids, and support my favorite charities. But all of these assignments, whether they generated income or not, made me feel good. They gave me a lot of satisfaction.

- They allowed me to engage with others around obligations and accountabilities.
- They let me use my gifts to serve others and solve problems.
- They helped me to define new expectations for my post-career life.
- They helped me reshape what I wanted to be in my post-career years.
- They helped me script my new life.

These assignments and activities also kept me busy. Very busy. They took a lot of time. The commitments piled up. All of a sudden, in the space of a few months, I didn't have time to go sailing, read books, or drive over to the university to have dinner with my kids and catch up with their lives.

After just a few months of retirement, I was hit with a cold, dark reality: I was more scripted than before, busier than ever, and it wasn't all good.

First, I had less control over my time, so this generated resentment that I had lost considerable freedom, and that I had done this to myself.

Second, the demands on my time were less predictable than they were before I retired. In my new roles, I was not the leader, manager, director, or conductor; I was the advisor, staffer, firefighter, or fixer. This uncertainty and lack of control generated a certain amount of stress. It was stress I could handle, but it was irritating, in part, because, once again, I had done it to myself.

Third, the freedom of choice and flexibility that I coveted – to do what I wanted to do when I wanted to do it – quickly evaporated. Every time I said yes to something, I reduced my degrees of freedom as more and more days got scheduled. It wasn't long before I was boxed in. More correctly, I had boxed myself in.

In short, now that I was retired, I was busier than ever, with token compensation, and, for the most part, not having fun, negating two of my three objectives. Indeed, I was doing all kinds of things that I would rather not be doing, but I had said yes too many times, in fact to everything. Why? I think it was because responding in the affirmative to opportunities for engagement was the way I knew I was still real. I had walked into a new life with my eyes wide open, but blind as to what it would mean, what purposes it would serve, or what consequences it would have, and I was unreflective. Shame on me for that.

After six months or so, I found myself in North Carolina sitting in the Bill Bridges workshop on transitions noted earlier, by chance not by plan. It was a fortuitous journey because that's where I learned of the need for individuals (like organizations) to make sure the transition process includes a *time-out* to step back, reassess, redefine, and rethink where they've been and where they are going before they reboot. That's when I realized that gliding into my post-career life on autopilot was not smart. That's when I recognized I needed to take a time-out to think about what I wanted to be, to do, and to have in the next phase of my life – and what I wanted to be needed to come first:

- not whether to relocate, downsize, or stay put;
- not to do a financial plan;
- not how to manage my money;
- not whether to buy gold or equities;

- not about nutrition, what foods to eat or vitamins to take;
- not what fitness routines to take up;
- not what pastimes I should adopt; and
- not to produce a bucket list of all the things I want to do before I kick the bucket.[61]

Instead, I needed a time-out to think about what I wanted *to be* in my post-career life and for what *purposes* and to what ends I should be using my gifts – and especially the gift of time.

In short, I needed to assess where I was in my life. Had I served my purpose in life? How had my life mattered? Had I lived a meaningful life? Had I been a good person? Were there things undone that needed to be done? Were there issues that needed to be addressed? Holes to patch up? New horizons to explore? Clearly, it was time to push the reset button, tidy up my life, make some amends, finish unfinished business, and chart a new course. It was time to take a mindful approach to rebooting for the final laps.

From a practical point of view, I needed a script, and for that I needed to revisit my calling and assess my gifts – both of which I had more or less taken for granted over the years.

It's clear many of us slip into a life of being what we do, where the doing comes first. We are parents, neighbors, and citizens. In our careers, we are lawyers, teachers, accountants, business men and women, traders, mechanics, farmers, factory workers, or carpenters, and so on.[62]

The late Henri Nouwen, a prolific author on matters of spirituality, calls these "doing" labels cultural illusions that can prevent us from facing up to what we want to be, and what we want to be is the most important. Nouwen explains it like this:

> "Cultural illusions fill the world in which we live and profoundly influence how we feel about ourselves. They [falsely claim]: You are what you *do* (lawyer, mother, CEO, teacher, care-giver, scientist, unskilled laborer), so do something relevant! You are what you *have* (wealth, education, power, popularity, handicap, nothing), so get busy and acquire all you can! You are what others think of you (kind, mean, saintly, loving, stupid), so act properly and gain respect!

> We are treated endlessly [in movies, art, and enter-
> tainment] to visions of people who don't know who
> they are, acting out their dreams for acceptance ...
> [But] we are not what we do. We are not what we
> have. We are not what others think of us ... [we are
> the] child of a loving Creator."[63]

So, whether we are spiritual, secular, or a person of faith (as Nouwen
was), our first challenge is to decide what we want *to be*. What we
want to be comes first – and then comes what we want *to do* (e.g.,
work, play, study, travel, relax) and what we want *to have* (e.g.,
from material things like a car or a fishing boat, to peace of mind
and a low golf handicap), discussed in detail in Chapter 16.

If we are lucky, we know who we are and have spent our career
doing what we are; we have been following our calling, so we can
continue that kind of work in some form in our post-career life. This
happens a lot. Consider the following, which I received in an email
from a good friend I'll call Joe, who had just reviewed an early draft
of this book.[64] He wrote, "I like your idea that retirement is greatly
over-rated, especially for those for whom their work is their calling.
A lot of people get great satisfaction from working. My own father
is a case in point." He continued:

> Dad worked as a machinist all of his life. A humble
> immigrant with a seventh grade education, he was
> very proud of supporting his family and doing his
> job. But his work and the commute were increasingly
> a struggle, so, at my mother's urging, he decided to
> retire at age 66.
>
> The day following his retirement, we honored him
> with a retirement party ... just family and close per-
> sonal friends and neighbors. Following the toast and
> accolades from around the table, Dad came over to
> me and said, "If you don't help me find a job, I will
> die." At first, I thought he was kidding but soon real-
> ized he was dead serious.
>
> The next week I called a friend of mine who owned
> a small offset printing business and lettering shop.
> That's the way he would describe it, but to me he
> owned machines ... and Dad was a machinist. A few
> days later, I brought Dad over for a "look-see." After
> surveying the situation, Dad told my friend, the

business owner, that he could maintain and repair the machines and make the parts necessary to keep the machines moving, helping the owner to avoid costly repairs and replacement parts. The business hired Dad the next day, and he delivered.

But there is more to the story. It turns out that the son of one of the business owners took an interest in the machine shop Dad had set up for the owner. Soon Dad, now working three days a week, was a machinist and a teacher. He became "Pops" to all in the shop – a name he loved. He worked at his new job for about five years before his health failed. He later told me, "Looking back, those were the best five years of my life and my career."

Joe's dad was fortunate. His job as a machinist was also his calling, work that not only allowed him to be productive but also brought him great satisfaction. On the other hand, many of us will reach the end of our career and conclude that our job or our career has not permitted us to express who we are. Or we might conclude that we've had a good life but we need to step back and rethink what we want to be in our post-career years and let what we do and what we have flow from that.

In either case, our post-career life gives us a second chance to let our authentic being express itself in what we do and what we seek to have.[65] And the center of gravity of what we do should be some combination of good deeds and good relationships with family, friends, and our fellow human beings – what the person of faith would call good works and love.

But how does this approach really fit with the idea of retirement? Does this retirement thing really make sense? The answer is no. Retirement is not natural. It is not historic. It is not healthy. It is not, for most people, fulfilling. For many, retirement is a widow-maker. Let's see why.

CHAPTER 6

RETIREMENT IS A BAD IDEA

"Retirement is the ugliest word in the language."
– Ernest Hemingway

"...the notion of retirement makes people old."
– Psychotherapist Penelope Russianoff[66]

"All the evidence points to the fact that retirement to
a life of leisure at 60 or 65 is ... suicidal."
– Marie Beynon Ray [67]

"If you rest, you rust."
– Actress Helen Hayes[68]

"I believe the word retirement in a decade will be a quaint,
charming term that people used to use."
– Larry Minnix[69]

Not all ideas are good ideas. Some ideas are bad ideas. Retirement is one of those bad ideas – it makes no sense. Bill Marriott of Marriott Hotel fame calls retirement a disease.[70] Publisher Malcolm Forbes said, "Retirement kills more people than hard work ever did."

Retirement is surely a dead-end idea – literally. Retirement is also a recent idea, and a pretty depressing idea at that.

Look it up in the dictionary. My Oxford [71] says to retire is to:
- withdraw
- go away
- retreat
- give up
- seek seclusion

The Oxford definitions include "retiring from the world" or "to retire unto oneself" or to become:

- unsociable
- uncommunicative
- withdrawn from society

Other lexicons use words and phrases that reflect the same ideas as withdraw, retreat, and a host of other behaviors that most in American culture would consider bad or undesirable.

How in the world did retirement and disengagement come to be viewed as desirable? More astonishingly, how did disengagement come to be something to seek, something to be valued, and something to be proud of once attained?

How many times have you heard people say, puffed up with pride and an apparent sense of accomplishment, or satisfaction, or admiration:

- "I retired early."
- "We are working hard and saving so we can retire early."
- "Did you hear that Dave and Jessica are taking early retirement? Wow!"

Indeed, there are literally dozens of books in your local Barnes & Noble that encourage early retirement or semi-retirement and provide advice on how to do it. These range from *The Complete Idiot's Guide to Retiring Early* to a testimonial that screams out that "Bob Clyatt realized there was more to life than 'just this'...and entered semi-retirement at age 42 and never looked back."[72]

Let's examine how we got so screwed up in our thinking about later life. Understanding how retirement ideas and practices evolved during the last century will make it easier to understand why the retirement culture is the way it is today and where it is headed in the years ahead.

First, **retirement is an invention of the modern world**; indeed it is largely absent from the ancient books of wisdom.[73] For example, retirement is mentioned only once in the Judeo-Christian scriptures. It is found in the Old Testament – referring to the Levites[74] who worked in the temple:

> Men twenty-five years old or more shall come to take
> part in the work at the tabernacle, but *at the age
> of fifty, they must retire from their regular service*

and work no longer. They may assist their brothers in performing their duties at the tabernacle, but they themselves must not do the work. This, then, is how you are to assign the responsibilities of the Levites.[75]

So historically, to retire was not to disengage or withdraw. Indeed, the script for later-life followers of the ancient scriptures called for men to "retire" to community service – by assisting their brothers in performing their duties at the tabernacle.[76]

However, community service is clearly not at the core of the contemporary concept of retirement. Instead, core elements of the modern notion of the ideal retirement that are reflected in today's media seem to emphasize:

- **Relaxation** – a carefree, stress-free, hassle-free life with limited responsibilities beyond the activities of daily living.[77]
- **Leisure** – a way of life with lots of free time for hobbies, sport, and other recreational activities because you are not only free of the obligations of employment, but also of lawn care, home maintenance, and many other requirements of domestic work.
- **Security** – life in a gated, age-restricted retirement village has come of age and is not like your mother used to know. Many now have limited access portals with key cards and video surveillance and sometimes even security guards, in-ground collapsible traffic-teeth, and electronic connections to each living unit.[78]
- **Self-indulgence** – think of the bumper sticker, "We are spending our kids' inheritance."
- **Dreams of unending pleasure** – for example, one ad calls retirees to participate in "... a little slice of paradise with sunshine and golf galore."[79]

How did this relaxed and carefree view of later life come about? A lot has to do with the intersection of three trends:

- greater longevity, which led to more years in later life,
- changing laws and practices that encouraged retirement by incenting people to quit working, and
- a pension to fund life in the bonus years.

Increasing longevity was perhaps the greatest human achievement of the 20th century, as life expectancy increased by two-thirds (from 47 years to 77 years) between 1900 and 2000. In addition, people were not only living longer, they were leaving their jobs or careers earlier, thus spending more time in later life.

DRIVERS OF LONGEVITY

Longevity is perhaps the greatest achievement of the 20th century. From the beginning of Man's time on earth until 1900, Man's life expectancy increased by about 30 years. From 1900 to 2000, it increased 30 years. [300] The shift has been dramatic:

Year	Life Expectancy
1776	35 years old
1800	36 years old
1900	47 years old
2000	77 years old
2010	78 years old
2020	79 years old

People are living longer and better lives. Indeed, there are now more than 60,000 Americans 100 years old or older!

There are many reasons for improvement in longevity in the 20th century. These include:[301]

- **Improved public health policies and programs,** including healthier mothers and babies, fluoridation of drinking water, vaccinations, tracking of epidemics, and control or eradication of killer diseases, such as small pox and tuberculosis.

- **Breakthroughs in medical care and treatments,** such as pre-natal and infant care, and joint and organ replacements.

- **Discovery of miracle drugs,** such as penicillin, insulin, streptomycin, cortisone, polio vaccines, and hormones, leading to dramatic decreases in deaths from killer diseases.

- **Healthier lifestyles,** including less smoking, safer and healthier foods, improved hygiene, and wide use of vitamins.

- **More safety consciousness,** as shown, for example, by safer workplaces and the dramatic decrease in automobile fatalities, both in absolute numbers and measured by miles driven.

At the same time, we experienced increasing urbanization as factory work displaced farming. In 1880, for example, 50 percent of men age 65 and over were living on a farm; by 1940, the number had fallen to 22 percent. At the beginning of the 20th century, farming accounted for more than 40 percent of the jobs and fewer but five percent at the end. In short, later-life Americans were rapidly migrating to new places and transitioning to new jobs.[80] This led to major disconnects as people moved from:

- traditional callings – working the fields, raising animals – to new factory or office-based vocations;
- home-based business – the farm, ranch, or cottage industry – to working away from home;
- gradual phasing out of the workforce – as the farmer reduced his part of the work of the family farm – to an abrupt exit from the urbanized factory or office-based workforce marked by a retirement party or a pink slip; and
- traditional support systems – the extended family and neighbors – to self-sufficiency or help from the church, charity, or government.

Thus for many, the bonus years were now characterized by abrupt transition from work and a collapsing support system. This meant later-life security was no longer assured, and people needed income to support their daily living after leaving the world of work.

Enter the modern concept of the pension – both the private pension and the government pension. The private pension is rooted in the economics of labor-force management that developed in the 1930s. That's when, in return for long service to the factory or the business, a corporation would give you a pension – in the form of a monthly retirement check (called a defined benefit) for the rest of your life. But it was a benefit with a condition, a quid pro quo: In return for the pension, you would agree to leave your job at 65, or some other agreed-to age. Thus the private pension was an effective incentive to retire older, slower, less nimble, and higher-wage workers, who could then be replaced by younger, faster, more productive, and less expensive workers.[81]

The other is the government pension.[82] America's first universal government pension was Social Security.[83] This new federal pension, beginning in 1935, provided financial support for a new class of later-life retired folks who could now begin thinking about the long vacation for two reasons: First, the price of leisure plummeted in the 20th century, and second, the costs of later-life leisure could be covered by the employer-provided private pension, supplemented by a government pension (i.e., Social Security) and the retiree's own savings.

COST OF LEISURE PLUMMETS

Many forces combined during the last century to reduce the cost and increase the consumption of leisure in America. First is **public policy**, as governments at every level invested more in national parks, state parks, marine sanctuaries, and local recreation facilities, such as swimming pools, bike lanes, jogging paths, ball parks, tennis courts, and the like, where access is free or affordable.

Second, **transportation technology**, especially the automobile but also the railroad and more recently cheap air travel, greatly increased access by average Americans to beaches, mountains, national parks, and other far-away places that were previously accessed primarily by the well-to-do or those who lived close by.

Third, **communications technologies**, the radio, followed by television, and now the Internet, have greatly increased access and affordability of all kinds of entertainment (music, sports, film, etc.), bringing it into the home and thus making it more accessible to older Americans who are homebound by finances or frailty.

Fourth, these electronic and **digital technologies** have broken the link between time and location on the one side, and the consumption of entertainment on the other. This new anytime, anyplace access to entertainment – including DVDs, TiVo, Netflix, and on-demand TV and films – affects everyone. But the largest beneficiaries are undoubtedly low-income and later-life Americans, who can now enjoy the best of Broadway free or at a low cost from the comfort of their own living room, or wherever they keep their TV or their home computer.

Each of these developments has increased the market for and driven down the cost of consuming leisure and recreation, and each has dramatically changed how and where we spend our leisure time.[302]

After WW II and during the nifty fifties, the retirement idea morphed into the Golden Years, where you live in blissful happiness playing golf all morning, card games in the afternoon, and watching TV during the evening. But the contemporary idea of the Golden Years is primarily a commercial concept of the mid-20th century, brought to you by Del Webb, a true visionary who developed the first modern retirement community, Arizona's Sun City, an innovation that became the model for a movement.[84]

So yes, retirement is now part of our culture. It seems as though it has been around forever. However, just as the concept of a *pension* is an invention of the late 19th century, the modern practice of *retirement* is an invention of the 20th century. Both have been in a constant state of redefinition over the past 100 years.

THE "LONG VACATION"

The idea of the long vacation has roots in the 1930s in something called the **Townsend movement**. In 1933, during the early years of the Great Depression, Dr. Francis Townsend, a retired California physician, proposed a guaranteed income plan that would give $200 per month pensions (more than twice the earnings of the average worker at the time) to all Americans over 60, "provided they spend the money within a month of receiving it." Though this was an early example of a bottom-up economic stimulus idea, Townsend also argued that it would give the elderly "time to enjoy life and gain the full advantage from recreation, political, and civil life, and have time to travel and get fresh viewpoints without keeping their noses to the grindstone."[303] Enter the idea of the Golden Years.

Townsend was no friend of FDR, and many say that the Townsend movement helped spur FDR to establish Social Security in 1935, although the monthly payments of what was then called old-age assistance was only $20 per month, about one-tenth the pension proposed by Townsend.

Today, there is a new upheaval around retirement. The pension plan model is changing. The corporate defined-benefit plan is being rapidly replaced by a defined-contribution plan, such as the Individual Retirement Account or 401(k).

In addition, America's growing government debt is raising many questions about whether retiring boomers can rely on the government's promise of a Social Security pension, and many state and local government pensions – for police, fire fighters, and teachers, for example – are also in trouble. Indeed, more young people today believe in UFOs than believe the government will honor its

Social Security obligations. Hence, we are once again in the middle of rethinking retirement, as later-life Americans are living longer, healthier lives, and growing numbers of Americans of all ages believe the government's pension promises will not be kept.

As a result of broken promises by government and the Great Recession's negative impact on savings and investments, many now in their late forties and early fifties say they do not expect to retire until their early seventies. Indeed a recent study of employee retirement preparedness revealed a majority of American workers will not be able to afford retirement until 73 years of age.[85]

As a result, today's later-life Americans are struggling to:
- absorb the damage inflicted on their nest eggs by the dot-com bust of 2000 and Great Recession that began in 2007, [86]
- adapt to increases in the retirement age – from age 65 to age 67 for those born in 1960 or later,[87]
- anticipate the many changes that are likely in pension and health care rules of the game,[88]
- deal with the social and financial implications of healthy longevity – i.e., living longer and living healthier,
- confront the family and financial implications of lingering illness and dependency,
- work longer in their careers, especially as work opportunities arise out of the increasing demand for talent and know-how in the workplace, and
- prepare for a new job (or career) as they retire, leaving their old jobs behind.

While government and politicians haggle on these issues, and financial planners work to keep up with volatile markets and changing rules of the game, **more Americans are coming to the view that old ideas of retirement don't make sense.** In fact, growing numbers are now gradually downshifting into their post-career years – much as the farmer or the home-based business owner used to do in the last century when younger family members came to take on more of the responsibilities of the enterprise.

Downshifting, where you move gradually and mindfully into your post-career years, makes a lot of sense. I didn't recognize it at the time, but downshifting was the strategy used by my parents years ago when I was a teenager. We lived in Indiana at the time, but my parents decided they wanted to relocate to the west coast of Florida when the time came for them to retire.

The story goes like this: My father, a senior executive in a mid-sized company that manufactured fireproof safes for homes and businesses, had many hobbies and interests and no intention of transitioning to a life of leisure. Similarly, my mother always had a full schedule of activities as a volunteer at the school, in the church, and with young women's groups, and she also planned to stay engaged after retirement. My parents decided to use our annual family vacation trips to Florida to explore locations until they found a place they liked. They settled on Fort Myers Beach, located on Estero Island. Soon after, they bought a modest beach house that needed a lot of work. By this time, my parents were in their forties, long before retirement. They fixed up the beach house a little every year during our vacations.

Then in their mid-fifties, about 10 years before retirement, they started going to Florida for three weeks instead of two. The three became four and then five weeks, taking leave time to made sure that they were doing the right thing, that Estero Island was the right place, and that they would have the opportunities they sought to make their new, post-career life work for them.

My father, an engineer by training, was a planner and list-maker. Somewhere during this transition, he decided he wanted to work in his post-career life, so he and my mother were planning to set up a fix-it repair shop or perhaps buy a local hardware store once they sold the family home up north. During all these years, they had made many new friends in their adopted community. They were involved in a local church and had relationships with physicians, pharmacists, pastors, and plumbers and all the other service providers that are part of life in a community. In the meantime, other members of our extended family also decided to retire in the general area of Fort Myers. So, things were coming together.

Looking back on their experience and how they managed their transition through later life, I think they did everything about right.[89] They planted roots 30 years before retiring, then down-shifted for about 10 years before actually separating from work, not unlike what people used to do many years ago – moving gradually out of the world of work and gradually into a post-career world, continuing to live in a way that would allow them to help others and make the world a better place.

CHAPTER 7
WORK TILL YOU DROP

"I prefer to be carried out of the place in a box."
- Father Bob, a Roman Catholic priest in Australia be-
ing forced by the Archbishop to retire at age 75.[90]

"I would rather wear out than rust out."
- Bob Hope[91]

"The aging man should neither stop working nor retire. Leisure
is even more dangerous for the old than for the young."
- Physician and Nobel Laureate Alexis Carrel[92]

"For the first time in human experience, we have a chance to shape our
work to suit the way we want to live instead of always living to fit in
with our work... We would be mad to miss the chance."
- Charles Handy[93]

"The race is over, but the work is never done while the power to work
remains... For to live is to function. That is all there is in living."
- Oliver Wendell Holmes[94]

"They found that the most powerful predictors of life satisfaction right af-
ter retirement were not health or wealth but the breadth of a person's
social network."
- University of Michigan Study[95]

"Could we please make it a six-year contract, since it would
be a shame to stop at 99."
- Leopold Stokowski to CBS at age 94[96]

Question: If we retire retirement, what do we do instead? Work? All our lives?

Answer: Yes. With a little luck and a proper attitude, we will die with our boots on.

Here's the plot.

Until the beginning of the 20th century, most people did not retire. They worked, and then they died. True, they would often down-shift, working fewer hours as the years advanced, but they almost always worked until they were disabled by frailty, illness, accident, or death.

One reason people did not retire is because work was a family af-fair – clearly so on the farm, where nearly half of all Americans worked in 1900.[97] But work was also a family affair for many who lived in cities and towns. Think of the butcher, the baker, and the candlestick maker. The butcher typically operated the family-owned corner grocery store.[98] Urban-based cottage industries in-cluded the baker and the candlestick maker. Many if not most of these vocations were home-based businesses.[99]

On the farm or in the urban cottage industries, it was taken for granted: All family members would tend to the work that had to be done. Since there is always work to be done on a farm or in a home-based business, people worked until they were sidelined by sickness, general physical deterioration, or frailty, regardless of age.[100] Hence, in the traditional, home-based economy that existed along with the emerging new economy of offices and factories, people were scripted until they reached frailty. In fact, in this set-ting, age was considered an asset – because of the wisdom, know-how, and stored-up experience that go with it.

Put another way, **work, until recent years, was an integral part of every chapter of life** – of the rich and the poor, young and old, urban and rural. It was a time when most people worked because there was visible work to be done, and they did it willingly as a productive member of the family enterprise. So before the modern age – when we exchanged work for pay and worked outside the home in an enterprise owned by another – it was through work in a family enterprise that later-life Americans stayed connected with family and friends, pursued their calling, and continued to be engaged with others in the activities of everyday life, including making things, mining things, or growing things.[101]

A lesson for us today is that **work should not be separated from the rest of life**. Indeed, work is an integral part of life. Yet, in our post-modern society, we tend to compartmentalize everything – as in the dreadful phrase work-life balance. Instead, work should be viewed as an integral part of – in harmony with – our whole life, because work is such an important part of the daily activity that binds us to others and to the common good, in addition to whatever other social or financial benefits we get from working.[102]

In the past, separation from work, (i.e., retirement,) was for the overwhelming majority of people measured in weeks or months, not years or decades. Most people died on the job or after a short illness. What we now know as lingering death – a prolonged period of progressive illness and disability preceding death – is a trend of the late 20th century and a pattern we have come to expect as normal.

Dr. Joanne Lynn, physician and respected health policy guru, points out that just a few generations ago, serious illness arrived with little warning, and people either lived through it or died quickly. In fact, life was mostly short for most people, serious illnesses and disabilities were common at every age, and dying was quick. Today by contrast, *growing numbers face lingering death*, which imposes huge financial and psychological costs on the family and growing financial pressures on the public treasury. [103]

WORK TILL YOU DROP: THE CASE OF GRANDMA MOSES

"I look back on my life like a good day's work, it was done and I feel satis-
fied with it...life is what we make it, always has been, always will be."
– Grandma Moses

Some people, when faced with disabilities, don't quit; they just shift to a new line of work more compatible with their limitations. There are many, of course, who have made a healthy adjustment to their limitations – Helen Keller and Franklin Roosevelt come to mind – and some Main Street characters I have met in my life.

Perhaps the most inspiring example is Anna Mary Robertson Moses, better known as Grandma Moses, one of America's most celebrated folk artists. Called "spry", "indomitable", and "mischievous" by the *New York Times* obituary, Grandmas Moses was born before Abraham Lincoln was president and died at age 101 when John F. Kennedy was president. She started working at age 12 as a hired girl doing housework. After marrying at age 27, she worked the family farm with her husband. She later switched careers again, creating and selling embroidery work, but was forced to give it up in her early seventies because of arthritis.

In 1936, at age 76, Grandma Moses began serious painting. According to the *Times*, "She could not hold a needle, but she could hold a brush, and she had been too busy all her life to bear the thought of being idle." Three years later, in 1939, Grandma Moses' paintings were represented in an exhibition of contemporary unknown painters at the Museum of Modern Art in New York. The rest is history. When she died in 1961, after more than 1,000 paintings, President Kennedy said, "...her paintings restored a primitive freshness to our perception of the American scene." [304]

We may be returning to a work-till-you-drop culture. For example, polls of later-life Americans show growing numbers are beginning to re-examine and re-value work as a post-career option – for many different reasons, including:

- **financial need** – as they watch their 401(k) and other investments that were planned to cover their post-career life evaporate in the stress of economic hard times.

- **boredom** as they begin to question time spent in endless rounds of tennis or golf or stamp collecting. Even playing sports and pursuing hobbies can be boring after a while.

- **desire to leave a legacy** – what psychologist Erik Erikson called *generativity* – reflecting a concern for the future of others that usually develops during middle age and especially a need to nurture and guide younger people and contribute to the next generation.[104]

- **psychological or spiritual need to work** – a need to be useful, to keep busy, to make the world a better place, or to leave our part of the world as least as good if not a little better than we found it. [105]

- **need for engagement** with others. People, after all, are social beings. We are not designed to live in isolation; we were not created to do nothing. Indeed, modern medical and social science research shows continuing social engagement is the strongest single predictor of successful aging.[106]

THE NEED FOR ENGAGEMENT IS IN OUR DNA

That Man is a social being is found in the secular texts – from the Greek philosophers (e.g., Aristotle) and Enlightenment thinkers (e.g., Kant) to America's history (Tocqueville) and modern social science (Max Weber) and commentary (David Brooks) – where Man is viewed as cooperating with others to meet his daily needs. In the ancient scriptures, God looked at his creation and said, "It is not good for man to be alone" and so he created a companion, woman. The story is found in Genesis 2:18-25. The rest is history.

I have come to accept the view that work is for man and that our calling is to work in some capacity as long as we are able. I began to think about this several years ago when I reconnected with Tim O'Reilly, a long-time friend going all the way back to middle school.[107] Tim always wanted to be a cop, but even more, he would often say that he felt he had a duty to serve. After serving five years as an enlisted man in the Air Force and 25 years in the local police department, he took the retirement package. After a month of travel and three months of relaxation, he came to realize that something was missing. "Once more," he told me, "I felt that duty was calling." But this time it was the local volunteer fire department. They needed more volunteers and were recruiting new members. Tim decided he would give it a try. So he volunteered to go through the training and make himself available whenever needed. He soon discovered that the ranks were greatly reduced during the day when most members were working at their full time jobs. Tim, now retired, could fill that void. Once again he was following his calling to serve.

My life experience tells me what Tim has also discovered – that work is a primary way to help others and make the world a better place. Work is a way to be fruitful and a primary source of satisfaction. Regardless of your worldview, my guess is that reflection will show that your calling is also to work – in some capacity – even during your post-career years.

CHAPTER 8

WORK-LIFE INTEGRATION

*"...what it means to lead a life that matters should at least begin
with the question of our livelihood."*
– Schwehn and Bass [108]

"Work is love made visible."
– Kahlil Gibran, The Prophet

*"We were not meant to take it easy. We were meant to struggle. The adolescent notion of unending play does not appeal to the mature mind.
It is, ironically, unending work ... that is more likely to keep us alive to a
ripe old age."*
– Marie Beynon Ray [109]

*"What would I retire to? ... When the good Lord wants me to retire, he will
take care of that. I work as much as I want ... the most wonderful thing
in the world is doing something you love to do."*
– Ray Charles [110]

*"... successful aging means giving to others joyously whenever one is able,
receiving from others gratefully whenever one needs it, and being
greedy enough to develop one's own self in between."*
– George Vaillant [111]

*"I know that there is nothing better for men than to be happy and do good
while they live. That everyone may eat and drink, and find satisfaction
in all his toil – this is the gift of God."*
– Ecclesiastes 3:12-13

*"In work, the person exercises and fulfills in part the potential inscribed in
his nature...Work is for man, not man for work. Everyone should be
able to draw from work the means of providing for his life and that of
his family, and serving the human community."*
– Catholic Catechism [112]

Work comes in many forms. Work is more than a job. We need to clarify our thinking about work as we enter the post-career chapter of later life. For example:

- What is work?
- Why do we work?
- What does our work do for others?
- How does work benefit the larger community?
- What does work do for us?
- What are the different types of work situations?
- What kinds of work should we consider?

If we think about **work from a secular perspective**, work involves purposeful and productive activities, both mental and physical. Work is an activity to which people devote their time, talent, and energy on a regular basis, a pursuit that yields a beneficial result for themselves, those around them, or the larger society.[113]

If we think about **work from a spiritual perspective,** we find many of the same characteristics. This should not be a surprise, because secular mindsets often reflect spiritual worldviews that are deeply embedded in the history of a culture. For example, writer and theologian John Piper says, "...at the heart of the meaning of work is creativity... if you are human, your work is to take what God has made and shape it and use it to make him look great."[114]

Thus, a spiritual concept of work is that work is made for man – not man for work. The mistaken idea that man is made for work would include everything from slavery to workaholism. That's not the healthy view of work we are talking about here. The spiritual also see work as purposeful, a view expressed in most secular perspectives. However, the Judeo-Christian notion goes a step further, targeting a specific purpose of work – which is to glorify God, or in John Piper's words, "make him look great."

Again, according to Piper, "When God commissions us to subdue the earth – to shape it and use it – he doesn't mean do it like a beaver. He means do it like a human, a morally self-conscious person who is responsible to do his work intentionally for the glory of his Maker."[115] It is this specific purpose that separates the work of humans from the work of beavers, hummingbirds or bees. Though these creatures work hard, subdue their surroundings, and shape them into dams, nests, and beehives that serve useful purposes, the biblical mandate to human beings to work is to serve a higher purpose.

Looked at from a Judeo-Christian perspective, work well done has a moral dimension. Reason: **Work is both a form of worship and a form of service**. In fact, the ancient Hebrew Scriptures use the single word *avodah* to express all three ideas: work, worship, and service.[116]

This *integrated* view of life – where life includes work, that work is made for man, and that work is good – is part of the heritage of western civilization. It is a view we may know in theory but do not honor in practice, for example, when talking about so-called work-life balance.

Work-life balance is a post-modern, fragmented view of life that rejects the idea that work is made for man and the idea that all work is important, regardless of what kind of work we do. The philosopher Kahlil Gibran, one of the world's most widely read poets, reminded us in *The Prophet* that "work is love made visible."[117]

Reformation leader Martin Luther said "all work is holy work." Dr. Martin Luther King said it best in kitchen-table English:

> "If a man is called to be a street sweeper, he should sweep streets even as Michelangelo painted, or Beethoven composed music or Shakespeare wrote poetry. He should sweep streets so well that all the hosts of heaven and earth will pause to say, here lived a great street sweeper who did his job well."[118]

So work is not just toil and drudgery. Work is, first and foremost, a blessing that provides an opportunity for us to serve, seek excellence, and achieve results for ourselves, those we love, and the larger community. Work is not just something we do for pay. Work is not just a job. Work is not something we do only outside the home. Work is anything we do where the result is to answer our calling, serve others, or make the world a better place, whether it is sweeping streets, preaching sermons, caring for the infirm, building a car, teaching school, laying bricks, painting fences, fixing the plumbing, or pounding nails.[119]

THE IDEA OF WORK IN HISTORY

Most ancient philosophies looked down on work. The Greeks, for example, thought manual labor was degrading and saw work simply as a means to an end, and often unpleasant means. "The goal of any refined person was to rise above it, to escape the need for it, and to spend one's time in contemplation."[305] Instead, according to ethicist Gilbert Meilaender, the classical perspective considered friendship, not work, as the primary source giving human life its meaning and significance.[306]

Early Christian thinkers, by contrast, imagined two levels of work – first-class and second-class, sacred and secular, higher and lower work.[307] This idea of a hierarchy of work came from the fourth century A.D., when church historian and polemicist Eusebius of Caesarea made a distinction between what he called contemplative work (or holy work) and active work (or vocational work – what you and I would call a job).[308] You had to do contemplative work or church work to do holy work – and, of course, holy work was more highly valued than vocational work. Put another way, the priest trumped the plumber in the culture of the early Church.[309]

The idea of higher and lower classes of work was rejected by the Reformation, in a discourse by Martin Luther, published in 1520.[310] Luther, the Protestant leader, challenged Eusebius and the prevailing Catholic view of work, a view that shaped the way people thought for more than a thousand years. Luther argued persuasively that **all work is holy work**. Luther said **work is a blessing**. He said we are to work, each of us, and to be good stewards of creation, which includes both service and the enjoyment of creation.[311]

As a result of Luther's new vision of work, people were uplifted, drawn by the new culture to create their own enterprises and engage vigorously and purposefully in trade and investment. The butcher, baker and bricklayer now viewed themselves as doing holy work, and when you are doing the Lord's work day in and day out, you will, for sure, do it with enthusiasm and be less likely to slough off. This new culture of work came to be called the **Protestant work ethic**, marking a major change in how ordinary people (i.e., non-clergy) thought about work. And by some accounts, the new culture of work also fueled the Industrial Revolution.[312]

Another Martin Luther, Dr. Martin Luther King, also a man of the cloth, said it best using contemporary terms:

> "If a man is called to be a street sweeper, he should sweep streets even as Michelangelo painted, or Beethoven composed music or Shakespeare wrote poetry. He should sweep streets so well that all the hosts of heaven and earth will pause to say, here lived a great street sweeper who did his job well."[313]

King's views echoed those expressed more than 20 years earlier by British novelist and Christian essayist Dorothy Sayers who said:

> "The Church's approach to an intelligent carpenter is usually confined to exhorting him not to be drunk and disorderly in his leisure hours, and to come to church on Sundays. What the Church should be telling him is this: that the very first demand that his religion makes upon him is that he should make good tables...Let the Church remember this: that every maker and worker is called to serve God in his profession or trade – not [just] outside it."[314]

So, from Martin Luther to Dr. Martin Luther King and from Dorothy Sayers to Dorothy Bass we are left with the view that all work is holy work and worship is not just for Sunday. If work is also worship, then worship is also for Monday and Tuesday and Wednesday through Saturday.

JUSTICE HOLMES AND LIFE-LONG LEARNING

The idea of life-long learning is brought to life by a story told of US Supreme Court Justice Oliver Wendell Holmes, Jr. (1841-1935). "When he reached 90, it became customary to ask him if he would soon retire. 'I shall not resign or retire,' Holmes reportedly said, 'until the Almighty Himself requests.'" Subsequently, Holmes did resign from the Court in 1932, but he didn't really retire. Shortly after his inauguration in 1933, the new president, Franklin D. Roosevelt, paid a visit to Holmes, now age 92. He found Holmes reading Plato. "Why do you read Plato, Mr. Justice," the President asked. "To improve my mind, Mr. President," Holmes replied.[316]

Second, **work is about obligations** – where you are accountable to someone to perform – as you are in the factory or the office, but even as you are in the home-based family enterprise typical of earlier times and making a comeback today in the form of home-based businesses. Having obligations and accountabilities is a condition I call *"on the clock,"* which I will discuss in more detail in Chapter 10. In the meantime, let's just say having obligations and accountabilities is important because it means you are engaged with others, which is not only a key to successful aging but also to long-term happiness:

> "People who commit to relationships are much happier than those who don't...When people commit to something that's...difficult to get out of, they report feeling happier." [120]

So, if work is about obligations and accountabilities, you may ask, "What's the definition of obligation?" Answer: Something that's hard to get out of because of a commitment, promise, or vow by which you are bound, ethically, legally, or morally.[121]

Third, **work comes in many flavors.** In my conversations with so-called retired people over the past two years, I have found that *most are working in some capacity*. Defining work in terms of obligations and accountabilities, the work "retired" people are doing seems to fall into one of **five categories of work,** described below and summarized in Figure 2.

1. **Paid work**. Surprising as it may seem, many in later-life still work for pay, earning a salary, wages, or fees. Employees work for salaries and wages; professionals, craftspeople, consultants, and freelancers typically earn fees. For many, especially knowledge workers, paid work in later life will often mean continuing to work as a lawyer, accountant, or pharmacist but often on a reduced-time basis. For others, it may involve work totally different from earlier career-related activities. For example, some years ago, a family friend and his wife retired to Florida. He spent the last half of his working life in middle management in a large corporation in Indiana – as what the Japanese would call a *salaryman*. After a few months in retirement, he was bored to tears (and his wife felt as though someone had intruded on her home life, a place she controlled for over 40 years of their marriage). Rather than cursing the darkness, he took up a part-time job sacking groceries in a local supermarket. Reason: This job provided a schedule, a chance to work with others, and an opportunity to provide a needed service. The additional income, in his case, didn't change his standard of living but was icing on the cake, along with the restoration of a more normal relationship with his wife.

2. **In-kind work**. I found some post-career Americans who trade their time for in-kind benefits, such as managing a condo or house-sitting in return for living quarters, serving as an usher at sporting events in return for watching the game, working on a cruise ship (e.g., as a lecturer or child-care provider) in return for passage, or providing clean-up services at a performing arts center in return for free tickets. In some cases, like managing the condo, you are on-call 24/7 with many obligations and accountabilities. In others, such as clean-up services, there is a lot more flexibility, where you may work only two to three times a week for four to five months a year, but the activity is scheduled and obligatory and involves accountabilities to others. It is work.

3. **Volunteer work.** Many later-life Americans perform "gift work"[122] – i.e., provide a benefit to another *on a regular basis* without pay or other consideration, usually through a non-profit organization. Volunteers may create *products*, such as knitting sweaters for the less-advantaged, casting pottery for sale at fund-raisers for the church, building a house for Habitat for Humanity, or manufacturing benches

for a neighborhood park. Volunteers more typically provide *services*, such as reception services (meeting, greeting, answering phones), helping to manage the Sunday church service, delivering meals on wheels for a local nonprofit, coaching a Little League baseball team, or providing free management assistance to a small-business owner or entrepreneur as a volunteer counselor for SCORE (Service Corps of Retired Executives). In these cases, charities, community institutions, or other nonprofits get the benefit of your time and talent, and you get the many benefits of social engagement, especially the opportunity to use your gifts to help others and to work to repair the world or make it a better place.

4. **Samaritan work.** Person-to-person care-giving or assistance arranged informally is something growing numbers of later-life Americans are doing for relatives, friends, or other loved ones. Samaritan work includes care-giving for infirm or frail parents, an ailing spouse, dependent neighbor or good friend – or when grandparents provide child care for grandchildren of working parents. It also includes personal services, such as rehabilitation assistance or assisting with the activities of daily living (ADLs), including food preparation, shopping, or transportation to appointments. It may be maintenance services, such as lawn care, gardening, shoveling snow for home-bound neighbors, or home maintenance assistance to later-life friends and neighbors who still live at home but can't do the heavy lifting to maintain and repair buildings and grounds.[123]

5. **Enrichment work.** Some may be surprised that I would include *enrichment* as work. But I discovered that many later-life Americans take a highly *disciplined approach* to self-improvement,[124] which I consider work in the spiritual sense we are talking about here. Examples of a disciplined approach to self-improvement include training for competition (e.g., amateur tennis, club golf, or Masters swimming); enhancing, sharpening, or applying a skill (e.g., woodworking, computer publishing, photography, chess, piano); learning something new, such as a new language, a new musical instrument, a new culture, a new body of literature (e.g., Chinese history, dynamics of aging, nutrition, or the history of baseball) or joining a book-reading club; creating, as in arts or crafts (e.g., playing the guitar in a country music group, portrait or landscape painting, writing, cartooning, carving), philanthropy,[125] or other activities

"undertaken for the love of work itself."[126]

The important issue here is that "enrichment work"[127] is not just messing around, pursuing a pastime, or something you do when you don't have anything else to do. If you go out to the courts a couple of times a week just to bat the ball around or read a book now and then – that is what we call a *pastime* or *leisure-time activity.* There is nothing wrong with leisure-time activity, but it does not qualify as enrichment work.

Activities qualifying as enrichment work are *planned* and *purposeful* (e.g., improving knowledge or performance, or applying skills to creating something or helping others) and involve obligating yourself to the process and making yourself accountable to someone (e.g., your spouse, partner, friend, or co-worker who knows of your commitment) who will help and encourage you to be true to your undertaking.

The frequency or intensity of work is not the issue. We may work every day. We may work one day a week or two afternoons a week. The important thing is to work, to use our gifts, to make ourselves useful to others, to improve our knowledge or skills, or to make the world a better place.

The income generated by work is not the issue. Work can be paid or unpaid and, according to a national survey reported in the MacArthur Foundation study on aging, "People rate unpaid work – child care, volunteer work, and informal help to others – as highly as paid work in terms of benefits to themselves."[128]

The motivation for work is not the issue. Motivation can have many sources – a need for money, a need to reduce boredom, a spiritual calling, a desire for enrichment, a need to engage with others, or the recognition that work exists for us to do. But whatever the motivation, *work is the surest path to continuous social engagement in later life.* And research on successful aging shows social engagement is strongly associated with good health and happiness and other measures of physical and mental well-being which, taken together, add up to successful aging.[129]

Some years ago, Lloyds of London reviewed retirement records over a period of ten years. The finding: **Those who retired early, died early; those who retired later, lived longer.** The Lloyds' conclusion: "They retire. They sit down for a while. Then they lie down. And then somebody carries them out."[130]

I'M STILL WORKING

Increasing numbers of men and women see later life, in the words of the *New York Times* reporter Kirk Johnson, "as just another stage of exploration and are pushing further and harder, tossing aside presumed limitations."[317] The *Times* story focused on Tom Lackey, an 89-year-old wing-walker who crossed the English Channel at 160 mph with his feet strapped to the top of a single-engine airplane.

To be sure, many later-life people are involved in the experiential world of sensation, adventure, and culture. But many are also engaged in work, such as many easily-recognized later-life notables:

- **entertainment personalities** – Clint Eastwood (80), William "Captain Kirk" Shatner (80), Regis Philbin (79), Sophia Loren (76), Robert Redford (74).

- **media performers** – *USA Today* founder and columnist Al Neuharth (87), *60 Minutes* reporter Mike Wallace (92), 60 Minutes commentator Andy Rooney (91), talk-show hosts Larry King (77) and NPR's Diane Rehm (74).

- **business tycoons** – Sumner Redstone (87), Warren Buffett (80), Rupert Murdoch (80).

- **entrepreneurs** – oilman and alternative energy evangelist T. Boone Pickens (82), former General Electric CEO Jack Welch (75) who started the Management Institute at Ohio's Chancellor University in 2009, Frank Hickingbotham (75), chairman and CEO of TCBY, which he founded in 1981 after his first retirement at age 45.

- **public service** – Michigan Rep. John Dingell (85), Hawaii Senators Daniel Inouye (80) and Daniel Akaka (80), Arizona Senator John McCain (74), former Federal Reserve Chairman Alan Greenspan (85), Senator Alan Simpson (78), co-chairman of President Obama's deficit-reduction commission, California Governor Jerry Brown (73).

- **nonprofit leadership** – former President Jimmy Carter (86) in Habitat for Humanity and the nonprofit Carter Center.

- **sports notables** – Nittany Lions football coach Joe Paterno (84).

- **fitness gurus** – Calvin Hill (76), Jane Fonda (72).

The alternative to boredom, deteriorating health, and isolation is to continue to work in some form, even after you retire. Justice Holmes, who worked into his nineties, said it this way:

> The riders in a race do not stop short when they reach their goal. There is a little finishing canter before coming to a standstill. There is time to hear the kind voice of friends and to say to oneself: The work is done. But just as one says that, the answer comes: The race is over, but *the work is never done while the power to work remains.* The canter that brings you to a standstill need not be only coming to rest. It cannot be, while you still live. For to live is to function. That is all there is in living. And so I end with a line from a Latin poet who uttered the message more than fifteen hundred years ago – "Death plucks my ear and says, 'Live! I am coming.'"[131]

Conclusion: It is important for us to work as long as we can – to have a finishing canter, hopefully to the end of life but certainly until the onset of disability owing to frailty, disease, or some other cause. This approach to our post-career years – engagement through work – is, in my view, the surest path to good physical and mental health and overall well-being in what should be the most interesting and satisfying period of our life.

Figure 2: Types of Work: A Summary

Types of Work	Full-time	Part-time
Work for pay Creating products or providing services for compensation.	Consultant; teaching; photography; desktop publishing; call center, store clerk; painting; carving; woodworking; care-giving in a nursing home; providing taxi or limo services; handy-man services.	Most everything that is full-time can be done part-time. More likely part-time for later-life people: gardening and lawn care; choir; music combo; baby-sitting/elder care; crafts.
In-kind work Trading time and services for in-kind benefits.	In-kind services tend to be performed on a part-time basis. A major exception would be 24/7 on-call property management services in exchange for free or reduced-cost living quarters.	Property management services in a condo; clean-up services at a sporting event; ushering at a symphony hall; parking cars at a restaurant; caddying or other services at a golf course.
Volunteering Providing a "gifted service" or benefit without compensation.	Volunteer services tend to be part-time – not because opportunities to volunteer full-time are lacking but because most later-life volunteers will choose to work part time.	Producing products such as knitting sweaters or casting pottery for sale at church or nonprofit fund-raisers, or building a house for Habitat for Humanity. Providing services such as reception services, Sunday church services, delivering meals on wheels, management assistance to a small business as a SCORE counselor.
Samaritan work Providing generous person-to-person care on your own to another.	Samaritan work tends to be performed on a part-time basis, usually without compensation. When Samaritan work is performed full-time, it is often for pay.	Care-giving for infirm or frail parents or child care for grandchildren of working parents; personal services, such as assisting with the activities of daily living (ADLs) including food preparation, shopping, transportation to appointments; maintenance services, such as lawn care, gardening, or shoveling w for homebound neighbors.

Figure 2: Types of Work: A Summary

Types of Work	Full -time	Part-time
Enrichment work Taking a disciplined and purpose-ful approach to self-improvement	With the exception of education to seek a degree or certificate, most people will undertake enrichment work on a part-time basis. When enrichment work is performed full-time, it is often for pay – such as the concert violinist, song writer, or painter.	Training for competi-tion in amateur sports (e.g., Masters swimming, tennis); improving a skill (e.g., digital photog-raphy, chess, desktop publishing); learning something new (e.g., mu-sical instrument or new language); or creating, as in the arts or crafts (e.g., song writing, sculpting, carving, painting, quilt-ing, pottery-making).

CHAPTER 9
WORK AND
LATER-LIFE SATISFACTION

*"The true secret of living is to keep busy. When you have all that time on
your hands, you think and act old."*
– George Burns[132]

*"Much research has shown that the most important predictors of vital age
are satisfying work and complexity of purpose."*
– Betty Friedan[133]

*"Far and away the best prize that life offers is the chance to
work hard at work worth doing."*
– Theodore Roosevelt

*"I cried because I did not have an office with a door, until I met
a man who had no cubicle."*
– Dilbert

**Opinion surveys confirm what we know from talking with friends
and colleagues: Some people are happily employed; many others
are not.** Fortunately, about half of us go through life in careers or
working at jobs that we like, that we find rewarding and satisfying,
but that means about half of us don't.[134]

Many of us got stuck in a rut that was not so satisfying. Sometimes we
were successful measured by income or position, but, truth be told,
most mornings we hated to get up and go to work. Reason: Our job
was not work; it was toil. It was drudgery. It was not our thing. It was
the pits, but we felt we were trapped by inertia or circumstances.

I was a lucky one. I spent most of my life in jobs I enjoyed, i.e., work
that was productive and satisfying. I think that happened because

my early life experiences forced me to come to grips with my calling, or what I was created to do.

I came to the view in my early twenties that my calling was teaching. Before going away to school, I had always wanted to be a lawyer.[135] However, I had an unexpected, thoroughly rewarding, and eye-opening experience as a teacher during my final year as an undergraduate at Knox College. From that experience I knew immediately that I wanted to spend my life learning and teaching. Here's what happened:

Each year the Knox political science department picked two incoming seniors to teach twice-weekly discussion groups for the introductory course in American government. I was one of the two selected in my senior year, and I loved the experience. I was stimulated by the way preparation for each class focused my thinking and reading. I found I had a passion to help students learn. I was thrilled by the experience of seeing some students get it – at least some of the time. And I found every part of the job to be both challenging and satisfying. Result: After about six weeks of performing my new part-time duties as a teacher, I jettisoned my plans from boyhood to go to law school. Instead, I rebooted to prepare for a life of teaching and learning.

After that, I went to graduate school and then spent nearly 20 years as a university professor – first at The Ohio State University and later at the University of Colorado and then at the Colorado School of Mines. During early mid-life, I did some career-shifting,[136] spending another (overlapping) 20 years as an association executive, heading groups that dealt with public policy or business policy issues. Even in those management roles, my job was really teaching.

Then over the next 10 years, I worked as a senior executive in a large corporation in the US and another in Australia, where my principal job (in public relations and government affairs) was advocacy, which, after all, is also a branch of teaching. Instead of the classroom, chalk boards, textbooks, and lectures, you use the media, advertising, lobbying, messaging, polling, and other tools of the trade to try to inform and shape the views of employees, vendors, shareholders, the public, and government regulators and policy-makers.[137]

Punchline: Every job I had over more than 40 years in several different arenas – higher education, association management, and corporate external affairs – enabled me to pursue my principal calling as a teacher and use my gifts as a communicator. I didn't plan it that way, but it worked out that way – and for that I was both fortunate and blessed.

At the same time, I've known many people, including good friends, who were not doing what they wanted to do – who wanted to be doing something different. Some had failed to discover their calling. Others had discovered their calling, but didn't have the freedom, opportunity, or audacity to pursue it.

By calling I mean what we do to fulfill our purpose for living – that is, working in a capacity we find both productive and satisfying. Here is the way Rick Warren, the widely-read author of *A Purpose-Driven Life*, described a calling in an interview on *Meet the Press*:

> "...each individual [was created] for a purpose...some are made to be oceanographers and some are made to be reporters...some are made to close deals...some are made to be accountants and some are made to teach school...How do you know what you're shaped to do? Two things: *it's fulfilling and you're fruitful*. If you're good at it and you love doing it, you come alive. You don't have to be paid for [doing] what your purpose is...Never give your life for money, because *your net-worth and your self-worth are not the same thing*. Your value and your valuables are not the same thing. And *who you are is much more important than what you do*. And if you can stop and look at your life and say, 'What do I love to do?'... Then that's the direction you need to head."[138]

A calling then is much bigger than a job. A calling reflects who we are, what we stand for, and to whom we answer. That dictates what we should do as we strive to live a life that matters.[139] We may pursue our calling in a paying job or in volunteer work. We may advance our calling in focused study, disciplined self-improvement, or even a serious hobby. We may find it working at home to produce something of value for our family or the larger community.[140] Whatever we do, we should make sure we serve our calling in some way, not the least in later life when we will have the most freedom to do so.

I had an early experience with *the difference between a calling and a job*. It shaped my thinking about work and vocations for 50 years, causing me to question writers and social commentators who seem to assume that your job is your calling – or that your job should reflect or be aligned with your calling. Many writers and social commentators also seem to assume that every job should be satisfying or meaningful (because, after all, theirs is), as if all people are supposed to get their fulfillment from their job (because, after all, they do).[141]

I'M GETTING BETTER, NOT OLDER

For many the later-life years are the best years. In *The Age Heresy*, authors Tony Buzan and Raymond Keene remind us that many of the world's "inspirational greats and geniuses" seemed to get more productive and creative as they got older.[318] Examples:

- Brahms was 43 when he began writing symphonies; his Fourth Symphony was perhaps his best.
- Leonardo da Vinci was 52 when he started painting the Mona Lisa.
- Michelangelo was 72 when he was appointed papal architect-in-chief of St. Peter's Basilica.
- Beethoven was sick, nearly deaf, and only three years from death with he wrote the Ninth Symphony, viewed by many as his best.
- Shakespeare wrote some of his most delightful plays late in life, such as *The Tempest* (his last).
- Mimar Sinan, the imperial architect of the Ottoman Empire, was in his eighties when he created his masterpiece, the Selimiye Mosque in Edirne, Turkey.

My personal experience was dramatic, in part, because I came from a family where most people did work at their calling. But I saw a very different picture when I was 18 years old, in the months before my graduation from high school. It was only years later that I came fully to appreciate the lesson of my experience.

It was 1957. I took a summer job at the Aluminum Company of America in Lafayette, Indiana. Known as Alcoa, the Lafayette operation was at the time the world's largest aluminum remelt and extrusion facility. The Alcoa plant took aluminum scraps – everything from used beer cans to discarded airplane wings – and produced recycled metal for new uses. It was the largest factory and the biggest employer in town. The wages and performance bonuses were good, also the best in town.[142]

I had one objective that summer: To make and save as much money as possible to help cover the expenses of my first year in college. I was assigned to an extrusion mill, where they pushed white-hot metal like toothpaste through a tube to make specialized shapes of aluminum – like for lawn furniture or automobile parts. The work was demanding, exhausting, hot, and dangerous. Still, I scouted around to find the most productive extrusion mill operator, the Top Gun, the guy whose team regularly earned the largest weekly bonus.

When I found my Top Gun, a mill operator named Jim,[143] I managed to get assigned to his team. I worked my tail off so he would keep me. I performed, and he asked the foreman to make me the permanent summer substitute of his team, as his regular team members were rotating off to take their vacation.

It was a good summer. Each week, I nearly doubled my hourly pay of $2.87 as a result of the bonus we nearly always earned working with Jim. At the time, I did not fully recognize the importance of my time with Jim and how much I was learning.[144]

As the weeks went on, I got to know Jim really well. He was a top performer and was respected by all, both his fellow union workers and foremen on the management side. One day I asked him why he didn't become a foreman and move up in the organization. He told me, as we worked away, that with his bonus and hard work, he could make more money as a press operator.

Then he said something that was a shock to a guy 18 years old, who had been taught that you should always aspire to be all that you can be. Jim said he had no desire to move up in the organization. He told me he worked only to feed his family and pay his mortgage because – and here was the bombshell – his real love in life was making old-fashioned pipe organs.

It turns out Jim produced hand-made pipe organs and had placed his creations in churches and music halls around the US, mostly in the Midwest.

I later learned Jim had also designed and built the family home with his own hands – a modest but lovely home on a hill with a commanding view of the surrounding region – with a workshop located behind the house where he hand-crafted his pipe organs.

Of course I was in awe of Jim, his impressive range of skills, and his no-frills, clear vision of his life. Jim was much like my father, who would come home in the evening and often, after dinner, retreat to his basement woodworking shop, where he crafted everything from home furnishings to grandfather clocks. My father, like Jim, was a craftsman. But Jim – unlike my father, whose calling was leadership in a mechanical engineering environment – had turned his calling into a home-based business.

Jim was a world-class craftsman. His calling was to build things with his hands, to build music machines called organs. Jim's job as the operator of an extrusion mill at Alcoa was not an expression of his calling. His Alcoa job was simply a means to an end – a way to augment his family income and even out his cash flow to pay the bills so he could devote his non-working hours to building organs, his first love and real calling.

Several years later, when I was reading a book by a professor who had never done anything outside the academic community, I found it hard to accept his disdain for boring, menial, and unfulfilling work, what he called dead-end jobs. I had learned from Jim that satisfaction in life, for many people, does not come from their job, but rather comes from what their job gives them the time, freedom, and money to do, such as building pipe organs.

More importantly, my experience with Jim taught me there are no dead-end jobs, just dead-end imaginations. Indeed, when there is work to be done, any job can be used, one way or another, to advance a calling or bring meaning to our life. We just need to figure out how to align our calling and our work with our job.

You can look at your work in many ways, whether you are in later life or not. Jim saw his daily work, his job, as instrumental to his life's work – a means to an end. This is only one of many ways we can think about our daily work.

Ways of thinking about work are shown clearly in the **parable of the bricklayer** – a story about five bricklayers taking a break and shooting the bull. The conversation goes like this:

- Bricklayer #1 asks, "Do you ever stop to think why we're all here laying bricks? I think about it a lot, and here's my take:

I've concluded that the only reason I do it is because my dad did it. He encouraged me to be a bricklayer, and he taught me the tricks of the trade. His dad, my grandfather, did it too. I'm not sure you can say family tradition is a good reason, but that's the tradition in my family and I think that's why I do it. What about you?"

- Bricklayer #2 says, "I do it for one simple reason. I do it to make money, to pay the mortgage, to provide for my family. If something better came along, I'd be gone in a New York minute."

- Bricklayer #3 says, "I do it because I like work where you can see progress every day. It's not like shuffling papers in some cubicle in a high-rise office building. That would drive me bonkers."

- Bricklayer #4 says, "I do it because I like laying bricks...I'm good at laying bricks. I enjoy it. I think I was made to lay bricks. Maybe it sounds funny, but I think brick-laying is my purpose in life. It's not something just anyone could do."

- Bricklayer #5 says, "I do it because – just look at what we are doing here – we are building a cathedral. I like being a part of something that's bigger than me, something that will last, something I can point to and say to my grandkids, 'I helped build that cathedral. That was my project.'"

In some circles, it might be fashionable to say bricklayer #5 is the one we should admire. But, in my view, all five gave good answers. Reason: Each of the five gave authentic answers, revealing that a sense of purpose drives why they go to work every day.

Even bricklayer #1, who appears to be driven only by family tradition – "I do it because my dad did it" – is giving the answer that most would have given in traditional society, where jobs are handed down through the generations, where fathers and mothers teach sons and daughters, and sons and daughters teach each other. Still, in each case, *each bricklayer gave voice to a purpose* – in each case a legitimate purpose – that can be expressed in terms of satisfying a human need:

- a continuity need – to maintain a family tradition (#1),
- a material need – to earn money, to achieve a means to an end (#2),
- a psychological need – to make visible progress in the work you do (#3),
- a spiritual need – to do something that uses your gifts to the fullest (#4),

- a transcendental need – to be engaged in something larger than yourself (#5). [145]

The only wrong answer from the point of view we are taking here is indifference: "I don't know why I lay bricks...I just do." That response, which no one gave, is unacceptable because indifference about the work we do is unacceptable. We should not accept the unexamined life.[146]

When you reach your post-career years, you have an opportunity to start all over again. If you terminate your career at 60 or 65, you will still have 10 to 20 years you can spend on the clock doing something fruitful that you also really enjoy. Most of us will have more than 20 years to work as we move through later life.

About a year ago, I met a guy at a service club meeting in Northern Virginia. His name is Frank, and I sat at "his" table. Frank is 83. He began his career in the Navy at age 18 and retired after 30 years at the age of 48. When he retired, he immediately went to work as a marine salvage consultant. He has worked in that job for 35 years.

As I was talking with my table mate, it came to me that Frank had spent more years in his post-career vocation, or retirement, than he did working in his naval career. He also told me he had made a lot more money in his post-career vocation. He tells me both careers have been satisfying, and in both careers he has been following his calling as an engineer, engaged in work that is both satisfying and productive.

Frank's life shows that some of us continue our calling and career into our post-career life. Others of us don't. One Christmas, visiting my parents in Florida, I connected with a fellow Hoosier from my parents' generation, a guy named Bob.[147] Bob had spent his life as a journalist writing for a local newspaper in Northern Indiana. He had a good pension, as did his wife, who also worked at the paper, and of course they also had income from Social Security. They were living comfortably, enjoying the warmer climate, daily walks on the beach, many new friends, and lots of leisure-time activities. But Bob was restless and told me he had been itching to do something useful.

That's where the surprise came in. I anticipated Bob would be going back to work writing a newsletter or doing PR for a local nonprofit, helping a charity raise money, teaching English for an after-school remedial program, or doing something that reflected his calling, experience, and skills as a writer and communicator. Instead, he decided to do something quite different. After casting about, Bob took a job ferrying rental cars for Hertz, that is, returning rentals dropped off at the Fort Myers airport to higher-demand points-of-origin (such as Tampa and Miami). He worked every Monday and then was on call during the week. He sometimes worked two or three days a week and loved it, because he was learning about a new business, making new friends in other cities among the Hertz employees, and finding relief from cabin fever, a relief, he said, his wife valued as much as he did.

Bottom line: There are many types of work to be done, and work can satisfy many needs, and not just the need of our calling. It is rewarding, I'm sure, when people are able to follow their calling in the work they do in their post-career life. That's why we cannot evade the fact that "what it means to lead a life that matters should at least begin with the question of our livelihood."[148] But work can bring satisfaction in many other ways for many reasons. So as we clarify how we think about and then script our later-life activities, we need to be clear about the role that work will play in that script.

CHAPTER 10

THE TWO-CHAPTER REBOOT

"Old age is 15 years older than I am."
- Bernard Baruch

"Change is situational...the new site, the new boss, the new team roles, the new policy. Transition is the psychological process people go through to come to terms with the new situation...Transition begins with letting go of something...Transition does not require that you reject or deny the importance of your old life, just that you let go of it."
- William Bridges[149]

"Not in his goals but in his transitions man is great."
- Ralph Waldo Emerson[150]

"[Later life] is like climbing a mountain. You climb from ledge to ledge. The higher you get the more tired and breathless you become, but your views become more expansive."
- Ingmar Bergman

Even though age 50 to the end of life defines the span of later life, nearly all of us will still be working at age 50, and most beyond 60. In other words, we will still be active in our career as we move into later life.

What is important about later life is not its span in years (which we can never know in any case), but how we use those years to make sure we finish well, whenever that may be. Therefore what is important is how we write the script for the chapters of our post-career life, however long or short they may be, whatever the span of years they may cover.

Some people talk about the chapters of later life. That's OK as long as they don't think about the chapters in terms of specific ages or years. Instead, we need to think about the chapters of later life in terms of who we are, what we do, and how we live them.

Later-life years that need to be addressed are those that come after we retire from our job or career, what I've been calling our post-career life. If we go by the statistics, the post-career years will, for most of us, begin at age 62, the average age when most Americans retire today. But regardless of the age, the day we retire marks the beginning of our post-career life. The question we need to be prepared to answer at that point is: *What do we do when our career is over but our life isn't?*

The answer I propose is the following: Invent a story line for your post-career years, beginning with who you are and what you want to do, then write the script and get on with it! That's what the rest of this book is about – a strategy for writing the script for the post-career years of your life. Here's how I've come to think about it.

When it comes time to retire, we need to take a time-out and then launch a reboot,[151] just as we do with a computer. When a computer quits working the way it should, we turn it off, wait a minute, and turn it back on. That allows the computer to reboot the operating system that makes it run. Or sometimes we buy new software applications, such as desktop publishing, expense tracking, or games, so we can make the computer serve *our* needs and work for *our* purposes. When that happens, we load new software and then reboot.

In the context of the transition to the post-career years, to reboot is to turn off the old life and then plan what we want to do next, after which we launch the new, post-career life. We do this by loading new software in the form of new (or, in some cases, renewed) objectives, priorities, and obligations that we will use to write the script for our new life. That's what I mean by a reboot.

There are two generic scripts for the reboot. Script 1.0 is used to outline our on-the-clock chapter; Script 2.0 is used to outline the off-the-clock chapter of our post-career life. Most of us should aim to use both scripts to tell the story of the rest of our life. This is what I call **a two-chapter approach to scripting our post-career life.**

As noted briefly in Chapter 8, *on the clock* and *off the clock* are ways of thinking about obligations and accountabilities. Being on the clock simply means you are accountable to someone to perform, that you have obligations and a schedule. Accountability can happen in a variety of on-the-clock situations. In my view, the most productive and satisfying on-the-clock situation is work.

Think back, for example, to **the five work situations** we described in Chapter 8, including (1) paid work, (2) in-kind work, (3) volunteer work, (4) Samaritan work, and (5) enrichment work. In each you have obligations and are accountable to other people. That's always the case when you are working for pay. But you also have obligations and accountabilities to others when you perform in-kind, volunteer, or Samaritan work, or take a disciplined approach to enrichment work. Thus when you have the health, mental capacity, desire, and will to take on obligations that will make you accountable to others, you are talking about a Script 1.0 story.

A Script 1.0 post-career story is primarily about engagement with others around mutual obligations and a negotiated schedule and accountabilities of some kind. It's about work. It is not how much time you spend on a payroll or volunteering or even what kind of work you do. The issue is having an obligation to perform and being accountable to someone for your performance.[152] That's why volunteer work such as mentoring a youth group, serving as an officer in a neighborhood association, volunteering as a business advisor with SCORE, or providing assistance to a church, synagogue, or mosque are all good examples of Script 1.0, on-the-clock work.

The ability to take on obligations and to perform on a schedule means that you have at least minimal physical abilities and mental capacity. It means you are able to get around, or at least to perform work if it is delivered to you, for example, by messenger or electronically. It means you can be independent.

Hence, a Script 1.0 later-life story is not about age; it is about your ability and willingness to perform on a schedule, and many can perform useful functions even when they are disabled and working, for example, from a wheelchair or scooter. The work depends on your talents, your will, and finding or creating an opportunity to perform. The schedule can take many forms, from full-time work to just a few hours a week.[153]

In fact, **most of us continue to spend at least some time working as we grow older**. In our fifties, most of us, more than 75 percent, work a standard 40-hour week or more. By the time we are in our late sixties, more than a third, about 36 percent, still work 40 hours a week or more. In short, as shown in Figure 3, as we grow older, the standard work week collapses as people tend to work fewer hours, but most of us continue working some hours each week.

Figure 3: "Work Week" Decreases with Age[154]

Age Group-> Hours worked per week	55-60	61-65	66-70
Under 10 hrs./week	3%	7%	12%
10-20	6	13	22
21-34	10	21	24
35-40	48	39	20
41-50	25	14	16
50+	5	4	1
Don't know/No Answer	3	1	6
Total	100%	99%	101%

Note: Numbers don't always add to 100% owing to rounding.

One of the most inspiring examples of a man who worked until the end and remained reflective about his personal life and involved in his professional life is psychologist Edwin Shneidman (1918-2009), a pioneer in the study and prevention of suicide. In 1958, Shneidman established the Los Angeles Suicide Prevention Center, a novel public health approach that was copied by more than 100 communities around the US during the next few years. In 1970, he joined the faculty at UCLA and was the founder of the American Association of Suicidology, the first professional organization devoted to the study of suicide.

Shneidman, the author of 20 books and many articles, was described in an obituary by Thomas Curwen, as "an indefatigable writer [who] advanced his own theories and perceptions about suicide, disarming most critics with wit, understatement and considerable knowledge."[155] In *A Commonsense Book of Death*, completed just before his own death, Shneidman reveals his never-give-up approach to life even as he is wearing out:

> "I am like an old Oldsmobile: one of my headlamps is broken, my differential isn't differentiating, my muffler has become muffled, my distributor won't distribute—and I can't buy replacement parts at Pep Boys."[156]

Still, despite his ailments, Shneidman worked to the end, writing what he called his own "pre-mortem" reflections on the latter stages of his own life.[157] Good for him – and for us too – that he wrote it!

A reader might say, "Well, it is one thing to work into your late eighties or nineties when you are a writer, like an academic or a journalist. But what about the rest of us, people who work the old-fashioned way by making things, growing things, mining things, fixing things, or moving things around?" That's a fair question, and that's why I've always been frustrated by retirement books that celebrate the later-life activities of writers, actors, preachers, politicians, and the well-to-do. That's why most of my examples are personal experiences I've had with Main Street Americans and what they do in later life. My later-life heroes are not Jimmy Carter, Warren Buffett, or Jack Welch types. These are people whose later-life transitions were more than helped along by high brand-equity names, gold-plated resumes, and rock-solid bank accounts. There are very few later-life Americans who can claim even one of these assets.

I am most inspired by successful later-life transitions of ordinary Americans who worked hard during their careers, raised families, and then found a way to navigate the shoals of later life to make a successful transition from their career to their post-career years. The key to success in nearly every case I've observed is not health, wealth, or location. Instead, **post-career success is achieved by purposeful involvement with other people** and engagement in a productive and satisfying activity.

One of my favorite examples is Ed Fergus. Ed was in the food processing business in Indiana, before retiring to Florida at age 61. After a few months in paradise, he decided to go back to work. He didn't need the money; he just wanted an opportunity to channel his time, energy, and talents – to make a contribution, stay engaged, and, he told me when I interviewed him, "to meet some nice people and help solve problems."[158]

I first got to know him as Mister Ed when he was in his early seventies. That's when he worked as the maintenance man at Dolphin Watch condominiums on Fort Myers Beach, Florida, where my mother lives. Mister Ed was the fix-it guy. He took care of the buildings and grounds. That was his job. But more importantly, Mister Ed took care of the people – with a smile, a wrench, 24/7 availability, and a solution for any problem. They all loved him, and he loved them back.

THE IMPULSE TO FINISH WELL

John Stephen Akhwari, the Olympic marathoner from Tanzania, is perhaps the most inspiring example of finishing well. The story goes like this. At 7:00 p.m. on October 20, 1968, only a few thousand spectators remained in the Olympic Stadium in Mexico City. It was cool and dark. The last of the exhausted marathon runners had been carried off to first-aid stations. More than an hour earlier, Mamo Wolde of Ethiopia, "looking as fresh as when he started the race," crossed the finish line, winning the 26-mile event.

As the remaining spectators were leaving, those sitting near the Stadium gates suddenly heard the sound of police sirens. All eyes turned to the gate. Along with the flashing red lights of police escorts, a lone figure wearing number 36 and the colors of Tanzania entered the stadium. His name: John Stephen Akhwari. He was the last man to finish the marathon.

Akhwari had fallen early in the race, badly injuring his left leg and ankle. Now, with his leg bloodied and bandaged with a T-shirt, he began his last lap around the 400-meter track, grimacing in pain with each hobbling step. The remaining spectators rose and the applause cascaded as he circled the track.

After crossing the finish line, Akhwari slowly walked off the field. He was immediately surrounded by reporters. A newsman asked Akhwari the question on everyone's mind: "Why did you keep going after you fell and were so badly injured and didn't have a chance to place?" His reply: "My country did not send me 5,000 miles to see me start the race. They sent me here to see me finish it. That was my mission. That's what I did."[319]

Mister Ed worked until last year when, at age 87, he gave up his duties after more than 15 years and went off the clock. Ed and Charlotte, his wife of 57 years, still live in Florida and are both actively engaged in life, but he is now spending more time with friends and family and just hanging out – and, he told me with a chuckle, "going to the doctor a lot." As we closed our conversation, Mister Ed said, "I don't really miss the work, but I sure do miss the people. That's why, every week or so, I go down to Dolphin Watch just to walk around and see how everyone is doing."

The stories of the two Eds – Professor Edwin Shneidman, always the teacher, and Mister Ed Fergus, who changed lanes[159] from a business man to a fix-it man and who took care of his people as well as their buildings – is really just one story. It **is a story of two men who loved their flock and worked to improve its well-being.** The professor did it through a life-long career of study, teaching, writing, and community service; Mister Ed did it first in the food processing business and then, in a post-career job shift where he worked in the trenches, day in and day out, to help people and make the world of Dolphin Watch a better place – having already performed his community service, first as a warrior and then as a POW in Germany in WWII.[160]

Another example riveted in my mind is that of Teresa Francis, a volunteer nurse I came to know when she was the social director in a retirement community. Her lifetime career, as a nurse, was and is a challenging profession. There are not enough nurses, and the workload is heavy. Still, she enjoyed her work. When the time came, she retired. However, after a few months she missed the psychic rewards of daily care-giving, and she especially missed her colleagues. One day while visiting her elderly uncle in a retirement community, she noticed a group of the residents in song and the woman who was leading them. The joy of residents was obvious on their faces. Teresa thought she would like to try this kind of work. Serving as a social director is not nursing, but like nursing, it is bringing comfort, joy, and stimulation to those who need it most. Soon after, Teresa started a new career as the weekend social director. The weekend schedule quickly expanded to working three days a week. In a recent email, she said to me, "This job is a delight. They love me, and I love them. I've never been happier."[161]

The lessons from these examples are simple: Whenever there's an opportunity to work in a job that is satisfying and where we can be fruitful because we have the talent, skills, and energy required to do it, then we should crank up our will to find a way to stay on the clock. **Engagement in some kind of work, at some level of effort, for as long as we are able, is another expression of our standing as human beings** and it is an opportunity we shouldn't pass up.

One of my Rotary Club friends is a guy named John Kenny. John was a pharmacist who retired when he was 65. John is now 88, but he still is on the clock. John lives in a place called Ginger Cove, an assisted-living community in Annapolis, where he chairs a men's group that meets weekly to hear outside speakers on politics, sports, economics, and culture. John lines up the speakers, briefs them on the group and what they want to hear, chairs the sessions, and generally holds the group together with a menu of activities that helps them keep up to date on cultural, public policy, and personal development.

John is also an amateur musician and plays the keyboard at the weekly meeting of the Annapolis Rotary Club. He says, "My fingers aren't as nimble as they used to be, but they still work." John is as busy as he was before he retired 23 years ago and clearly is still on the clock with a demanding weekly schedule and obligations to others – including his obligations as a newlywed.[162]

There is also Script 2.0, which I call *off the clock*.

Off the clock refers to that time of your life when you no longer desire, or have the ability, to be obligated and accountable to others. You no longer want to be on a schedule that requires you to perform somewhere or for somebody at a certain time on a regular basis. You decide to give up your post-career job whether it's paid work, volunteering, or the disciplined activity involved in enrichment work. You want – or need for health, peace-of-mind, or other reasons – to go off the clock to simply relax or to reduce the pressure that goes with work to perform, answer to someone, meet a schedule, be on time, and conform to a to-do list.

Being off the clock doesn't necessarily mean you aren't engaged. Indeed, many who go off the clock, like Ed Fergus and like my own mother, remain fully engaged, but their engagement is on their own terms. That's the difference – engagement is on *their* terms.

Indeed, many of those off the clock are still engaged in the activities of daily living (ADLs), [163] e.g., shopping, making and keeping medical appointments, preparing meals, putting out the rubbish, taking care of the car, and other ADLs that are involved in taking care of yourself and, in many cases, your spouse.[164]

Being off the clock can also include engagement in scheduled activities, including activities that bring high satisfaction, but they are considered off the clock activities, because (1) engagement is optional, not obligatory, (2) productivity is not an issue, and (3) you are the primary beneficiary, and not necessarily other people or the larger community. These kinds of off-the-clock activities include:

- **Organized games** – e.g., card-playing such as bridge, gin rummy, and sometimes even five-card draw if not Texas hold'em; board games such as checkers, chess, Rummikub; table games such as ping pong, billiards, dominoes; group exercise such as tennis, water aerobics, mall walking, golf outings; etc.

- **Organized events** – e.g., pilates classes, visits to museums or botanical gardens, group shopping, adventure travel, eco-tourism, scenic cruises, foliage excursions, book clubs, Bible study, picnics, cooking classes, etc.

- **Participation in solo or lone-wolf activities** – e.g., journaling, reading, writing, walking, biking, hiking, climbing, weight lifting, lap swimming, sailing, hunting, flying, bird-watching, or other activities that are typically done alone or in tandem.

This on-the-clock/off-the-clock way of thinking about later life came from a recent experience with my mother, who is 94. She has some ailments, like most people her age, but is generally in good health physically and sharp as a pistol mentally. My father passed away when she was 65, so she has been living alone, happily and successfully, for more than 25 years.

During that time, she has cared for herself and her household. Though she has deeply missed my dad and her husband of 43 years, she has been consistently and broadly engaged with friends and neighbors who live in her 32-unit condo and others on the north end of Estero Island. Perhaps more importantly, she is Internet-savvy, serves as the glue of our immediate family, and has remained connected with our extended family, on both sides, including nieces and nephews, and even grand-nieces and nephews.

Some of her relationships are fueled by periodic visits because she is fun to be with. It doesn't hurt that she lives on the beach, and hers is an enjoyable place to visit, especially in the winter. All her relationships are punctuated by connections such as annual birthday cards, periodic weddings, new babies, visits, and frequent email exchanges on the Internet.

For many years after my father's passing in 1982, my mother was active as a community volunteer in Fort Myers Beach. She was especially active in her church, working every Thursday to help prepare for the Sunday service and contributing to other faith community activities.

Then, a year or so ago, she downshifted out of her community activities – not her personal engagement with family and friends, but her scheduled community activities and hard-wired obligations. It was time, she said, to pass those obligations on to others. She was often tired and sometimes not feeling up to the tasks, and told me she didn't want to disappoint people by missing deadlines or ending up a no-show.

Mind you, she is still healthy, frisky, and fun to be around. She is still learning – in fact, just recently she learned to do video Skype, so we now "see" her when we call. But she no longer wants to be held to a schedule. In other words, she decided on her own to go off the clock. My mother is now in the second chapter of her retirement, following a Script 2.0, and she is still going strong. In fact, she still helps out at the church on Sundays whenever possible, but on her schedule.

A post-career story has nothing to do with where you live. You can continue to live at home in either condition – on the clock or off the clock. Like John Kenny, you might reside in an assisted living community and still live on the clock, because of obligations you take on and the accountabilities you have as a leader. At the same time, like many who live in retirement communities, you may continue to be deeply engaged with others, even though you have gone off the clock, because of all the scheduled activities that are offered to retirement community residents for their personal enjoyment. Or like my mother, you may continue to live at home and continue to be engaged, but off the clock. **It all depends on the level of the obligations and accountabilities that you are able, or choose, to have**.

Clearly, however, by the time people reach a nursing home, they will, by definition, be off the clock, unable to live independently, that is, unable to perform activities of daily living (ADLs) without help. But before that happens, many people simply get tired or worn out. That is natural.

But here's the point: **We should try to stay on the clock as long as possible**, regardless of our age or where we live. Let's recap the reasons:

The first is spiritual: There is work for us to do, to help others or to repair the world or make it a better place. As long as we are able, we should find it and do it. We may do it only one day a week, maybe even less, but we should work as long as we are able.

SOCIAL ENGAGEMENT AND THE RETIREMENT COMMUNITY

Cynics and social critics typically describe age-restricted retirement communities as age-homogeneous *cocoons*, *God's waiting room*, or worse. However places such as Sun City, The Villages, or assisted living offerings such as Sunrise Senior Living Communities work because they appeal to a later-life market that values safety, security, fitness, and leisure time opportunities. But, importantly, they also provide opportunities for purposeful social engagement, and that is a major core asset of a modern retirement community that contributes to successful aging.

Age-restricted communities that embody later-life values of safety, security, fitness, leisure, and purposeful engagement are found throughout the US, and also in Europe, Canada, and Australasia. For example, the Del Webb communities, which started the retirement community movement with a single Sun City, outside of Phoenix, now number more than 50 communities in 20 states. The assisted living model, originated by Sunrise Assisted Living, now has nearly 400 retirement communities in the US, Canada, the UK, and Germany. And there is a new wrinkle called *all-ages communities*, referring to retirement communities that are progressive, diverse, and located in more urbanized areas preferred by younger homebuyers.

I used to be agnostic about retirement communities. But over the past few years, I have watched my older relatives and more recently friends move to age-restricted communities. During that time, I have also been working on this book and learning more about how lifestyle choices drive so much of what we call successful aging. As a result, I have come to a different and much more positive view of retirement communities. Reason: The retirement village, with its many opportunities for fellowship and purposeful small-group activities around life-long learning, fitness, and spiritual growth, along with group approaches to some of the activities of daily living, provides an environment that encourages purposeful social engagement that is key to successful aging.

The second is quality of life: Working keeps us engaged, and research on what is called successful aging tells us that social engagement is the best path to living well in later life.[165] This is not about longevity, or how long you live. Successful aging is about

your quality of life and living a good life – one that provides fulfillment and a sense of being valued, cared for, and appreciated for
who you are and for the contributions you have made and are making to the well-being of others.

The third is fitness: When we work, we are more active, and that
helps us stay fit and gives an added incentive to be fit. And fitness is good, not only because it increases our quality of life, but
because fit people live longer, live better, and die faster.

Too many people today retire to a one-chapter, post-career story,
transitioning immediately from career to a Script 2.0 where they
begin living off the clock. That means they retire and then immediately reboot to an off-the-clock scenario of leisure or engage
in activities designed primarily to serve their own needs but not
necessarily the needs of others or the larger community.

Unfortunately, the one-chapter, Script 2.0 approach to post-career life has long been presented as the ideal retirement in the
media, in advertising, and in too many conversations among
later-life Americans. However, there is a healthy alternative, and
that is the two-chapter post-career story, one that begins with an
on-the-clock, Script 1.0 scenario and ends with an off-the-clock,
Script 2.0 scenario – i.e., to become a booter. Let's hope the two-
chapter booter approach to scripting our post-career years becomes the new normal, as the first of America's 78 million boomers
turn 65 in 2011.

CHAPTER 11
A SECOND CHANCE FOR ALL AGES

"It is never too late to be what you might have been."
– George Eliot

"Americans are coming to realize that the second half of life can mean a second wind...that we are not done at 60, not at 70, and maybe not at 90...[Instead] it's now a time to step up, to contribute, and serve, a time to learn and try new things. There is much behind, but there is more ahead."
– David Corbett [166]

"A person with a calling is a person who has purpose and meaning that will not end with the termination of a job. Those who are called will go and find new directions by virtue of how they are wired by God and what they're called to do."
– Howard Hendricks [167]

"When I stand before God at the end of my life, I would hope that I would not have a single bit of talent left, and could say, 'I used everything you gave me.'"
– Erma Bombeck [168]

"Men and women approaching retirement age should be recycled for public service work...We can no longer afford to scrap-pile people."
– Gandhi

I was privileged in my career to spend a lot of time living, working, and traveling outside the US – in Europe, Asia, Australia, and South America. When you live and travel abroad, there are many opportunities to gain a new perspective on your own cultural heritage as an American and to assess your cultural practices against those you encounter as a stranger in a foreign land.

Based on my experience, **the second chance is one of the most distinctive and admirable features of American culture,** and one of the most dramatic differences between American culture and those of the rest of the world. The second chance is something you don't read much about in the "blame America first" malaise that infects so much of what our political and media elites say and write these days, but it may be our most important cultural asset in accounting for America's exceptional success as a nation.[169]

Americans are great believers in the second chance. And the re-demptive second chance is built into our basic institutions. Indeed, many have observed that the American frontier was advanced by new Americans seeking a second chance and an opportunity for redemption as they headed for the frontier, forsaking custom, cre-ating new institutions and social practices, and sometimes even fleeing the law.[170] Over time, this frontier spirit has been embedded in nearly every aspect of American culture and is reflected in our institutions and in the ways people treat each other, both in their personal and professional life. [171]

Let me give an example from education. In America, education has been about citizen-based leadership, experimentalism connected to the changing needs of students and society, new possibilities created by new technologies, and decentralized flexibility.[172] These virtues have created some pretty good results over the past 150 years or so.

Compare this to much of the rest of the world, where you find nationalized school systems, centralized control by professionals, bureaucratized administration, a disconnect from the grassroots needs of society, and most disturbing, top-down, expert-driven, one-size-fits-all curricula with test-driven certification. Result: In Japan, the UK, and many other countries, your educational future is determined by the time you are 12 years old, often based on tests given in the sixth grade. The die is cast and, if you don't make it, well, that's tough.

Not so in America. In most places in the US, you have repeated opportunities to prove yourself.
- First, you go to elementary school.
- If you don't do so well there, you have a chance to start over,

with a clean slate, in middle school.

- If you don't do so well in middle school, you begin again, with a more or less clean slate, in high school.

- If you don't make high school grades that will allow you to go to the university, you can go to the community college and, if you make the grade, you can earn a vocational degree or even transfer to a four-year institution, taking your credits with you.

- If you don't make it there, you can go to a proprietary school such as DeVry University, Kaplan, or the University of Phoenix– or even an online or correspondence school – to learn a profession, trade or craft.

- If you don't make it there, well, you go to Craigslist or LinkedIn or some other source to find a job and go to work.

- And anywhere along the way, as long as you are 18 or older, you may decide to enroll in the American institution that spends more on education and training than any other – the US military.[173]

And it doesn't end there. Early on or even mid-career, you may decide to go back to school for a professional or technical degree, for example, at the community college, an American innovation where adult and continuing education are an important part of its mission, or to a proprietary (that is, for-profit) school, like the University of Phoenix.[174]

America is unique in this important way: Our institutions and practices recognize that the intellectual and social development of individuals varies widely from person to person. How many people floundered in high school but caught fire at the community college, graduated from a four-year institution, sometimes with honors, then mid-career, completed an advanced degree in business, public administration, or some other professional discipline? In fact, it happens all the time in America.

America is not just the land of the second chance. It is the land of the third and fourth and fifth chance. And the sixth and seventh. America is the land of redemption, where compared to other countries, it is hard (not impossible, but difficult) to get slotted by the system, and then written off. I'm not blind to the reality that some people do get tagged as low potential or typed as low achievers. But slotting people here is more typically a mistake, not an intentional act of academic policy, as it is in many other countries. [175]

In America, opportunities to make a mid-course adjustment or even start over are ever-present, at every stage of life. Indeed, **the idea of starting over is part of our cultural DNA,** and it doesn't stop with the young. The idea and practice of the second chance also extends into later life, if we just take advantage of our freedom to review our gifts, explore new on-the-clock options, and then join the booter nation, taking the leap into a two-chapter approach to a post-career life.

Chapter 12
Later Life and the Second Chance

"It is never too late to be what you want to be."
– Robert Dilenschneider [176]

"Once you're over the hill, you begin to pick up speed."
– Peanuts creator Charles Schulz

Our post-career later life presents a huge opportunity to recalibrate, and then to reboot, to try something new, explore paths not taken, or even start over. Later life is a time when you can invoke the American tradition of the second chance to script a fresh approach to the bell lap of your life.

Of course, we never know when we are on the last or bell lap. That's why we must be prepared every day to live in a way that will let us finish well. Unlike the Olympic marathoner, Tanzanian John Stephen Akhwari, who knew the finish line was 400 meters away when he entered the stadium in Mexico City, we can never know when we will be finished, because the finish line of life is not something that's knowable. But finished we will be. That much is certain.

On the other hand, we do know when we have reached later life. That's when we get "the letter" from the AARP. We do know when we have terminated our career, or had it terminated for us by a pink slip or thank-you letter, or a mandatory retirement. When that happens, we know our career is over but our life isn't. And when that day arrives, we still have choices about how we spend the rest of our life, whether it is measured in days and weeks, or years and decades. The plain fact is that our time is limited – like "a mist that appears for a little while and then vanishes" – but that also helps to focus our thinking and doing, especially as we move into our post-career years.[177]

In fact, beginning with the end of your life, whenever that may be, and working back to the present is a powerful way to stimulate your thinking about the choices you can make as you enter the post-career phase of your life. One way to do that is to work through the exercises in Kerry and Chris Shook's *One Month to Live*, an inspiring book that will bring what best-selling author Lee Strobel calls "new urgency, fresh purpose, and a sharper focus for your life."[178]

By this point in *Reboot!*, I hope you agree with me that retirement makes no sense. In fact, I think hotel magnate Bill Marriott got it right when he said retirement is a disease...and it will kill you faster than any job or volunteer assignment, especially if you have no script for the rest of your life. Without a script, your sense of purpose fades, your engagement with others diminishes, your talents and skills (like unused muscles) atrophy, and your disposition hardens.

Retirement is especially silly for those who are physically and mentally able to work or otherwise contribute to society, to the family, neighborhood, or community – and not just the one with trees and shrubs but also the online communities and social networks that provide opportunities to engage and to serve.[179]

Retirement is also a non-starter if we accept that our calling is to work – to help our neighbors and to repair the world or make it a better place. There may be some who think none of what we do here in this life or on this planet matters one way or another. But those people are a small minority. Indeed, Winston Churchill, when asked if he planned to retire after losing the post-WWII election in Great Britain in 1945, said, "Not until I am a great deal worse and the Empire is a great deal better." Six years later, at the age of 77, he was re-elected Prime Minister of Great Britain.[180] The ancient Scriptures give us the same story, telling us to "be fruitful and increase in number; fill the earth and subdue it. Rule over the fish of the sea and the birds of the air and over every living creature that moves on the ground."[181]

Even among those who are uncertain about their place in the cosmos, we know from experience that most will care about their legacy, and we know from surveys that most believe we are not alone. Most Americans also believe that somewhere in time and space there is an energy, or a God, or a spirit, or a Creator who made all this happen and brings order to the world, an order we have spent thousands of years trying to understand, especially since the Age of Reason and the discovery of the scientific method in the 17th century. [182]

Even among those who are uncertain about what comes next, most believe something comes next[183] and that it does matter what we believe and what we do while we are here. I count myself among those who are convinced that it matters, both what we believe and what we do, our faith and our deeds.[184]

You may have a different mindset.[185] However, whatever your mindset – call it a philosophy of life, worldview, belief system, faith walk, or religion – the chances are that you believe that you have an obligation, as they used to say in the US Army ads, to **"be all that you can be"** – to use your gifts to the fullest.

Whatever your philosophy, worldview, belief system, or religion, the chances are that you subscribe to the Golden Rule that we should treat others as we would like to be treated,[186] a view also expressed in the ancient scriptures as "Do to others as you would have them do to you."[187] Or even more simply, "Love your neighbor as yourself."[188]

Whatever your philosophy, worldview, belief system, or religion, the chances are you believe in good stewardship – the idea that you should take care of the world and, if possible, leave the world a little better than you found it. If you can carve a Mount Rushmore, build the Brooklyn Bridge, discover a flu vaccine, or invent the light bulb, that's good. But it also makes a difference, a big difference, when you:

- love and honor your spouse;
- encourage your kids, devoting time to shape their growth, nurture their development, teach them right from wrong, and give them opportunities in life;
- honor and care for your parents when they need you;
- work, because there is much work to do and the opportunity to work is a blessing; and
- serve your community, where raking the leaves or shoveling the snow in the clean-up brigade or hosting youth groups ranks with serving as an elected official.

Let's be clear: Each and every one of these achievements counts for loving your neighbor and improving the world, as most faiths,

philosophies, and guidelines for living, regardless of their differences, call us to do.

**Affirming our purpose in life and deciding what gives life mean-
ing is important.**[189] Purpose is important because when you com-
bine your view of your purpose in life with your assessment of
your gifts (time, talent, and treasures), then you are well on the
road to clarifying how you should manage whatever time you have
left. And for most of us, as we enter post-career life, we will count
the years in decades.

CHAPTER 13
LEADING A LIFE OF MEANING

"...the secret of man's being is not only to live...but to live for something definite. Without a firm notion of what we are living for, man will... destroy himself..."
– Fyodor Dostoevsky's Inquisitor in The Brothers Karamazov

"I have seen the meaning of my life in helping others to see in their lives a meaning."
– Viktor Frankl[190]

"The Buddhas do not tell the way; it is for you to swelter at the task."
– Dhammapada[191]

"The noblest question in the world is what good may I do in it."
– Benjamin Franklin

"If you want to lift yourself up, lift up someone else."
– Booker T. Washington

"To whom should a life that matters really matter?"
– Schwehn and Bass[192]

"Adding life to years; not just more years to life."
– Motto, American Gerontological Society (1955)

"...without meaning, men die."
– Viktor Frankl[193]

My father died when I was 43, three months to the day after he retired. It was an event for which we weren't prepared. My father was a picture of good health and always lively, engaged, and in good spirits, and he and my mother had well-laid plans for their post-career years together. So his untimely passing at age 65 was a shock to our family and led to an unexpected journey, especially for my mother.

In the days that followed, a friend who had lost his own father said to me, "You don't begin to live until your father dies." At the time, I wasn't sure what he meant by that. Still, the phrase stuck in my mind. It wasn't until the next couple of years that I began to understand what he meant.

For many of us, it's not until your father dies, or mother or another person very close who has played a large role in your life, that you begin to think seriously about your own mortality.[194] Until that time, you know there is an end, but the idea that our time is limited is largely an abstraction. One of the characteristics of youth is a sense of invincibility and immortality, and as you grow up you are too busy with the activities of everyday life to give much thought to the end, an event that seems way over the horizon.

But as we reach middle age, the reality of our mortality tends to occupy more space in our consciousness, especially as those closest to us begin to pass on. These otherwise sad events also have an upside. Indeed, increased awareness of our mortality can be a healthy development. To paraphrase Gandhi, the non-violent Hindu leader of Indian independence following WWII, "Think, dream and plan as if you will live forever; act as if you will die tomorrow."

The reality of a limited life is also central to the Judeo-Christian tradition. Pastor Rick Warren says, "...embracing your mortality sets you free to live a meaningful and satisfying life without regret."[195]

Man's recognition of what Freud called "the inevitable end"[196] is also important from a secular perspective. Psychologists like Erik Erikson tell us that the certainty of our demise focuses the mind and gives meaning to our daily life because we know our time is limited.[197] "So many Russians; so little time," as Ronald Reagan's defense policy guru Richard Pearle used to say, before the fall of the Berlin Wall.

Knowing that we will someday buy the farm (as my grandfather back in Indiana used to call it), we should focus our thinking and amplify the importance of today, which could be our last. But it still begs the question: What are we here for in the first place? What's this journey all about? Is it only to spend our time learning (school), working (career), playing (retirement), and dying? Or is there more? And if there is more, what is it?

THE GOOD DEATH

Psychologist Ed Shneidman (1918-2009), a giant in the world of thanatology – the discipline that studies the medical, psychological, and sociological aspects of death and ways people deal with it – was a professor at UCLA and a pioneer in suicide prevention. Professor Shneidman worked until the end, writing *A Commonsense Book of Death: Reflections at Ninety of a Lifelong Thanatologist*. An obituary by a close friend and protégé noted "...that he managed to meet all the ten 'Criteria for a Good Death' that he set forth in an article with that title published in June, 2007, just two years before his passing, in *Suicide and Life-Threatening Behavior*, the journal of the American Association of Suicidology."[320] Shneidman's Ten Criteria of the good death include:

1. Natural. There are four modes of death – natural, accidental, suicide and homicide (NASH). Any survivor would prefer a loved one's death to be natural. No suicide is a good death.

2. Mature. After age 70. Near the pinnacle of mental functioning but old enough to have experienced and savored life.

3. Expected. Neither sudden nor unexpected. Survivors-to-be do not like to be surprised. A good death should have about a week's lead time.

4. Honorable. Filled with honorifics but not dwelling on past failures. Death begins an ongoing obituary, a memory in the minds of the survivors. The Latin phrase is: *De mortuis nil nisi bonum* (Of the dead [speak] nothing but good).

5. Prepared. A living trust and prepaid funeral arrangements. That the decedent had given thought and made arrangements for the necessary legalities surrounding death.

6. Accepted. Willing the obligatory, that is, accepting the immutables of chance and nature and fate; not raging into the night; acceding to nature's nonnegotiable demands.

7. Civilized. To have some of your loved ones physically present. That the dying scene be enlivened by fresh flowers, beautiful pictures, and cherished music.

8. Generative. To pass down the wisdom of the tribe to younger generations; to write; to have shared memories and histories; to act like a beneficent sage.

9. Rueful. To cherish the emotional state, which is a bittersweet admixture of sadness, yearning, nostalgia, regret, appreciation, and thoughtfulness. To avoid depression, surrender, or collapse; to die with some projects left to be done; by example, to teach the paradigm that no life is completely complete.

10. Peaceable. That the dying scene be filled with amicability and love, that physical pain be controlled as much as competent medical care can provide. Each death is an ennobling icon of the human race.

To address the question of how to finish well requires us to ask some pretty fundamental questions about our life, such as:

- What is our purpose for living, our mission in life?
- What gives meaning to life?
- What is required to live a life of meaning?
- To whom does it matter that we live a life of meaning?

Life's meaning for most of us is a process of discovery. That's true whether we consider ourselves spiritual, New Age, or secular, and it is something most of us struggle with over a lifetime. Many try to bundle life's meaning in a neat package, but most of us don't buy it. We have to discover it on our own. Holocaust survivor and psychologist Viktor Frankl describes it this way:

> "Man's search for meaning is based on the tension between what one has achieved and what one still ought to accomplish, or the gap between what one is and what one should become...What a person actually needs is not a tensionless state but a striving and struggling for a worthwhile goal, a freely-chosen task...a potential meaning waiting to be fulfilled only by that person."[198]

Even when life's meaning is packaged in a way that its followers claim is divinely inspired – as in the Torah (Jewish), the Bible (Christian), the Koran (Islam), the Dhammapada (Hindu), or other sacred texts – we humans are often slow learners and typically spend many years of our life trying to unbundle the package so we can understand it. To stimulate our own thinking, let's consider different ways others have pondered life's meaning.

Viktor Frankl unpacks life's meaning into creative, experiential, and attitudinal values[199] that are expressed in the following three actions:[200]

- **What we give to the world,** measured in terms of **service** – work, deeds, and creative activities. Think of Martin Luther King's street sweeper or Dorothy Sayers' carpenter, noted in Chapter 8. Think of Ed Fergus, the maintenance man or Steve Jobs and Steve Wozniak creating the first Apple computer in a garage. Consider the Fortune 50 CEO establishing an academy to retrain workers, psychologist Ed Shneidman pondering his own dying and death and sharing it with us, the teacher teaching English literature, and a budding

Shakespeare writing it. Clearly, each of us gives to the world through our work, the work we've found, or been given, to do.

- **What we take from the world,** measured in terms of **relationships or experiencing things** – in both the natural and social world and in the world of artifacts. For one of the most moving accounts of finding spiritual meaning from experiencing artifacts, see the account of Henri Nouwen, theologian, author of some twenty books, priest, and teacher who resigned his tenured position as a teacher to became a full-time care-giver in a mental hospital. He reflected on his experience viewing the original Rembrandt painting of the Prodigal Son, at the Hermitage in St. Petersburg, Russia, an experience that changed his life forever.[201]

- **How we struggle,** meaning how we **confront the inevitable stresses and tragedies** of life, the heart-breaking events we cannot avoid and cannot change. Examples: death of a parent or child, loss of a spouse, unwanted pregnancy, divorce, incurable disease, inoperable cancer, permanent disability, loss of a job, loss of life-long savings, sterility, dementia or senility in a loved one – or, in Frankl's case, his struggle with the horrors of Auschwitz, the Nazi death camp where he was a prisoner during World War II. Do we confront life's realities positively and constructively, or do we confront them with a sense of despair and defeat? Do we see the glass half full or half empty?[202]

Pulitzer Prize-winning novelist John Steinbeck interrupts his narrative in *East of Eden* at Chapter 34 to discuss the purpose of life.[203] Steinbeck asks, "What is the world's story...and what's life all about"? His answer: Human beings have only one story and that is the struggle between virtue and vice and that we are caught up "in a net of good and evil."

Steinbeck's net of virtue and vice, good and evil, includes kindness and generosity as much as greed and cruelty. "A man," he says, "after he has brushed off the dust and chips of his life will have only the hard, clean questions: Was [my life] good or was it evil? Have I done well – or ill?" Steinbeck says this struggle forms a constant tension in the choices we make in our daily life, day in and day out. "I am certain," he says, "that underneath their topmost layers of frailty, *men want to be good and want to be loved*. Indeed, most of their vices are attempted short cuts to love."

His conclusion, however, is sobering:

> When a man comes to die, no matter what his talents and influence and genius, if he dies unloved his life must be a failure to him and his dying a cold horror. It seems to me that if you or I must choose between courses of thought or action, we should remember our dying and *try so to live that our death brings no pleasure to the world*.[204]

Put in a positive way, a life of meaning for most people – spiritual, New Age, or secular – is to seek to do good and be virtuous, to help others and to make the world a better place. We seek to be good and virtuous as much as we can in all that we do, in all the choices we make, and in all of our relationships, from the most casual to the most intimate.[205] In the words of philosopher Dallas Willard, we all have "a unique eternal calling to count for good in God's great universe." [206]

Jeff Sandefer is a successful entrepreneur. More importantly, he is an innovator in the world of business education. As the founder and hands-on leader of a trail-blazing MBA program at the Acton Institute in Austin, Texas, Sandefer promises that the Acton MBA will:[207]

- learn how to learn,
- learn how to make money, and
- learn how to live a life of meaning.

Based on more than a decade as a leader in business education, Sandefer observes that when graduates leave, most will have learned how to learn. After a few years, many will have made a lot of money. But when they come back after they've made it in the marketplace, most appreciate that Acton taught them how to live a life of meaning.[208]

How do you do that? Sandefer's advice to young people can also be applied to those entering later life. For post-career Americans, it would go something like this: As you approach the bell lap of your life, you will want to answer three questions:

1. How did I make a difference?
2. Was I a good person?

3. Whom did I love and who loved me?

These are terrific questions. And note that the answer to each of these questions requires us to look outside ourselves. Put another way, these questions tell us we are most likely to discover the meaning of our life in the way we interact with others and with events of the world that touch our life.

Each of us should ask those questions of ourselves as early as possible in our life, and on a regular basis. But often it takes growing older and the death of a loved one to bring us to the table. In any case, it is never too late to begin. And once we ask the questions, we should review the answers on a regular basis, say, at least once a year or as dictated by changes in our health, financial condition, or other events in our life.[209] We should do this for two reasons: First, keeping these questions in the front of our mind can lead us to do the right thing when we face new choices. Second, we should never give up on self-improvement and thus the opportunities to burnish the answers we can give.

Put in the form of declarative guidelines:
1. We should **strive to make a difference** until our dying day, even when that means graciously accepting the care others give to us.

2. We should **strive each day to be a good person,** regardless of our past failures. Every day is a new day. Every day we have a second chance to get it right, knowing that we will never fully succeed in getting it right.

3. We should **love, respect, and appreciate others,** just as we seek to be loved, respected, and appreciated.[210]

Life's meaning is not usually self-evident. For most of us, we come to know through our experiences in life. It's true that some find that life's meaning and purpose are delivered in whole cloth by something larger than ourselves, e.g., by God, the natural law, or a secular or spiritual guru. But even in those cases, one has to open the door and take it on board. Others find meaning in something beyond themselves, such as looking after an elderly parent, saving the environment, helping the poor, or teaching a child to read.

However in either case, "...meaning doesn't come from just believing in something larger than oneself; it comes from being in service to that something."[211] It's in this sense that, for most of us, life's meaning is something we discover by living, learning, loving, making choices, getting smacked down, reflecting, and beginning anew after false starts, dead ends, and cul-de-sacs.[212]

For the person of faith, life's meaning is informed or revealed by discovering and experiencing the transcendent, for example, experiencing God for those in Abrahamic religions (Judaism, Christianity, and Islam).[213] It may be a gradual process of enlightenment and confirmation. Or, it may be a sudden awakening, what some would call a "born again" experience.

- We see evidence of this process of discovery and revelation underway in churches, synagogues, and mosques around America.[214]
- We see it in silent retreats where we learn to listen, contemplate, and reflect.[215]
- We see it in small groups and in scripture studies where we are stimulated to use evidence and insight and exercise faith and reason so we can think spiritually, historically, and logically as well as analogically and metaphorically.
- We see it in experiences. These could be experiences in history, science, and poetry – each one of which can be a source of revelation. It could be in quiet moments of reflection or in the stress of a tragedy or great suffering.

If you come from the Judeo-Christian tradition, you quickly learn the question is not just "who are we" but also "whose are we." That's because **the Christian calling has three elements**: to love and honor God, [216] to serve others, [217] and to make the world a better place[218] – the idea that we should "contribute to the repair and progress of our society." [219] However, the first of these is first because our primary calling is to love God[220] and to honor him in all that we think and do: in our home, work, and play – in all aspects of our life, thoughts, and actions.[221]

The secular person might say, "That may be good for you, but it doesn't work for me." Fair enough, but consider the philosopher Leo Strauss, who observed, "...transcendence is not a preserve of revealed religion."[222] Indeed, **the transcendent is affirmed in most worldviews embraced by most human beings** as they try to understand man's place in the cosmos and thus life's meaning and why life matters.[223]

It is my experience from talking about these issues with friends and colleagues who are not of my faith – and more than a few with no faith at all – that nearly everyone asks basic questions about life's purpose. Most people, not all to be sure, believe there is a higher purpose and even a higher being or higher power of some kind. This view is also confirmed by opinion surveys.[224] Surveys also show that answers people give to life's purpose, at least in western culture, generally follow the same line of thinking for the person of faith as for the secular person or the person whose beliefs are not rooted in a specific religious or spiritual tradition.[225]

In short, **life's meaning for the non-religious also comes from discovery**, usually by the same process of exploration and trial-and-error that is the *modus operandi* of the person of faith. It's a process that gives the seeker ever-increasing understanding and self-knowledge that comes with living and learning. Like the person of faith, those who come from a secular or New Age tradition have their own creeds and scriptures that present beliefs, values, and ways of thinking. That's why New Age books of inspiration and related materials are among the best sellers in any Barnes & Noble.

Indeed, New Age philosophy also has guidelines for living. One example – certainly not the only one – is the widespread popularity and success of 12-step self-improvement programs. They also have a liturgy of rituals and practices. That's why you find a booming business in yoga, spas and "life-changing" retreats to nourish the heart and feed the soul. That's why thought leaders as different as Tony Robbins, Wayne Dyer, don Miguel Ruiz, and Steven Covey[226] are so important to so many people today – just as Dale Carnegie was a secular guru to many in the 20th century, including Warren Buffett and my own father.[227]

Whether you rely on ancient scriptures or on modern, widely read and popular authors, nearly all address the role of the transcendent in some way, and most help their readers and followers to live a life that matters. For example,

- Wayne Dyer is an effective and persuasive speaker, often seen on PBS television performing for fundraisers. Before a large group, you will hear him talk about a spiritual force he calls "the Energy" and you can see a round, lighted physical symbol of "the Energy" on the stage.[228]
- You can't get far into Steven Covey's *Seven Habits* before you suspect you are reading a thoughtful book written by a man anchored in a faith of some kind. In Covey's case, if you dig a little, you find the anchor of the Mormon faith.
- When best-selling New Age author don Miguel Ruiz urges his followers to "always do your best" and to "help me change

the world," he also says he has "no religion at all..." Still, somewhere in his thinking and reflection, he has found these two oughts: (1) to do your best, and (2) to change the world. He also affirms his belief in what he calls "the infinite" and the "the absolute" as "a living being and...we all are part of that living being."[229]

- When you read the 2010 edition of Richard Bolles' *What Color Is Your Parachute*, he reveals in an essay reproduced as Appendix A that his Christian faith has shaped much of his thinking and his overall worldview about vocations and job-hunting.[230]

However we understand our life's purpose and whatever the source of that understanding – in philosophy, religion, science, or experience – it is clear that we can benefit from trying to comprehend how we get meaning from our day-to-day life. The discussion above is simply a way to open the door to different ways of thinking about how we can make the most of the time we have left, in a purpose-driven life that matters.

CHAPTER 14
TIME-OUT TO SCRIPT A NEW LIFE

"Experience is not what happens to you. It is what you do
with what happens to you."
– Aldous Huxley

"It's not what happens to you, but how you react to it that matters."
– Epictetus

"If you don't change direction, you will end up where you are headed."
–Lao-Tzu

"I don't know what my resting heart rate is – and I hope I never do."
– Leslie Milk[231]

"The years between fifty and seventy are the hardest. You are always asked
to do things, and you are not yet decrepit enough to turn them down.
– TS Eliot

"Long I sought for the earth's hidden meaning;
Long as a youth was my search in vain.
Now as I approach my last years waning,
My search I must begin again."
– Johnny Piper[232]

You are now retired, or anticipating that day, close at hand, when you hang up your spurs, lock up your tools, turn in your keys, or clear out your desk to enter your post-career years, a time that should be the most creative and rewarding period of your life.[233]

When we retire, it is important to retire to something. Indeed, as the young John Piper wrote, "Now as I approach my last years waning, / My search I must begin again." With these words, John Piper captured a reality that has been lost over the past century in American culture, namely, we cannot retire to retirement. That makes no sense. Most of us are not going to withdraw, retreat, or seek seclusion, the common definitions of retirement. Successful aging is best achieved by continued social engagement, and **social engagement, in my view, is most naturally and effectively achieved by working,** full time or part time, either for pay or pro bono, as a volunteer, or in one of the other forms of work noted in Chapter 8. So let's examine how we should decide what to do with our gifts of time, talent, and treasure as we transition to our post-career years.

We know from research on transitions, that most people don't just move from Condition A (e.g., working) to Condition B (e.g., a post-career life) without going through some kind of transition. An effective transition is one that goes from A, to a time-out where we can think things over and plan what's next, and then to B, the new situation. [234]

The period we set aside as a time-out could be days, weeks, or months, but however long, **the time-out is where we let go of the old life and develop an image of the future.** The time-out is when we form a view or expectation of what is to come. The time-out gives us time to load new objectives, priorities, and obligations, and then to reboot so we can get on with our new, post-career life.

Change management guru Bill Bridges calls this time-out between A (what we were before we retired) and B (what we want to become post-career) a *neutral zone* – which is one of three stages of any transition. These include:
- The Ending,
- The Neutral Zone, and, after a pause,
- The New Beginning.

Understanding and embracing each stage can help us transition into a more meaningful, productive, and hopeful future.

What Bridges calls the neutral zone I call a *time-out*. This time-out may involve just a few days, or it may involve months. You may do it yourself, or you may have a coach or attend a workshop, seminar, or retreat to stimulate your thinking and keep you on track. However you choose to do it, the time-out is important because in this phase of the transition, we let go of or redefine the old and invent the new.

A time-out is not an interlude to take a breather, go fishing, or embark on that long-postponed trip to Paris or Peoria. It is not just doing nothing or doing your thing, or just relaxing – though a time-out may be well-served by an interlude to experience that long-deferred trek, cruise, RV trip, or vacation before getting back into the swing of things. But an interlude or a long-postponed vacation is not itself a time-out.

A time-out is a mindful process to review and rethink what matters in your life and set a course for the future. A post-career time-out is used to:

- **assess** your life so far, to examine your dreams, achievements, disappointments, likes, dislikes, what satisfies and what doesn't – and to consider remaining agendas or unfinished business;
- **take stock** of your treasure, your assets and deficits, your talent and skills – and especially how they square with new aspirations of your post-career life, including new agendas and unfinished business; and
- **decide** where and how you go from here – i.e., how you want to script your new post-career life and then get on with it.

Many of us will feel good about what we have achieved but will have a lot of unfinished business that we want to complete using the same talent and skills we have been using. In this case, the future will be pretty much like the past, and the time-out is likely to be short. Others of us will want to make a break with the past, chart a new course, or follow a path not taken. When that is our decision, our time-out is likely to be longer.

Long or short, we should use a **time-out to review five key questions:**

1. Have we achieved what we set out to do, or do we have unfulfilled dreams and aspirations? Do they still matter, or has their time passed? Do we have unfinished business that we want or need to complete? Are there amends to make?
2. Have we lived a life that matters? Are there areas where we could or should do more? How do we continue to live a life that matters in our post-career years, and what should our priorities be?

3. Do we want to explore new paths, learn new things, do new work, have new experiences, or acquire new skills we have not had the time for in the past?

4. Do we want to spend our post-career years in the same location and at the same pace, or perhaps move to a different place or seek activities with less intensity?

5. Do we want to create a bucket list of things to do before we kick the bucket – places to go, people to see, and things to do in the years we have left? The business concept applies here: "If you can't measure it, you can't manage it." In our post-career years, we might say, "If you don't plan it, it won't happen." That's where the bucket list comes in – to see the Grand Canyon, dive Australia's Great Barrier Reef, go camping in the mountains, visit your best friend from grade school, read the Bible – or Moby Dick, or The Brothers Karamazov – or fulfill some experience or aspiration that thus far is unrealized.

In other words, do we want to create a new story using new plots and new scripts? Do we want to start over? Or perhaps there are unfinished elements of our old script, issues that we need to go back and clean up.

Wherever we come down on this continuum of life satisfaction, the time-out is used to assess where we are, what we want to be in our new life, and what we are going to do next. Regardless of where we fall on the scale of life satisfaction many of us will want to stir up glowing coals that have been left untended, rekindle old relationships, and make amends where amends are needed. Others will make a bucket list of places to go, people to meet, things to do, or amends to make before we kick the bucket.[235]

Some will take a time-out and find a high level of satisfaction with their assessment of their past life. Others will decide there is more to do, more to achieve, and more to experience. This idea was captured by Mitch Albom in his best-seller, *Tuesdays with Morrie*. On one of his Tuesday visits, Albom walked in to find scraps of paper where Morrie had jotted down his thoughts about life:

> "He wrote bite-sized philosophies...'Accept what you are able to do and what you are not able to do'; 'Accept the past as past, without denying it or discarding it'... 'don't assume that it's too late to get involved.'"[236]

THE BUCKET LIST

The phrase "bucket list" comes from a wonderful film, a comedy about redemption, directed by Rob Reiner, written by Justin Zackham, and released in 2007.[321] *The Bucket List* is a story about corporate billionaire Edward Cole (Jack Nicholson) and working-class mechanic Carter Chambers (Morgan Freeman), both terminal cancer victims with nothing in common except their illnesses. While sharing a hospital room, Carter begins writing a bucket list, *a wish list of things he wants to do before he kicks the bucket.* Billionaire Cole finds the list, embraces the idea, and after some discussion, they escape the cancer ward together to head off on a road trip with their bucket list. In the ensuing days as they achieve one item after another, both of them heal each other spiritually, become unlikely friends, and ultimately find the joy in life they have both missed along the way.[322]

The bucket list in the film included:

1. Witness something truly majestic
2. Help a complete stranger for the good
3. Laugh till I cry
4. Drive a Shelby Mustang
5. Kiss the most beautiful girl in the world
6. Get a tattoo
7. Go skydiving
8. Visit Stonehenge
9. Spend a week at the Louvre
10. See Rome
11. Dinner at La Chevre d'Or
12. See the Pyramids
13. Get back in touch with an old friend
14. Visit the Taj Mahal
15. Visit Hong Kong
16. See Victoria Falls
17. Go on a safari
18. Drive a motorcycle on the Great Wall of China
19. Hunt the big cat
20. Find the joy in your life

Bookstores are packed with books showing many different approaches to a time-out assessment, but whatever approach we use, an established approach or exercises we invent, it is important to ask questions around how we use our **three most important gifts: the 3Ts of time, talent, and treasure.**

Most of us already will have considered questions around the 3Ts at various turning points in our life – if not during a past mid-life crisis, then perhaps when we left school for the world of work or lost a job or when the last of our children went off to college. But regardless of how often we have revisited these important questions, it is essential to confront them when we retire to enter the post-career phase of our life.

However, there are likely to be three big differences today, compared to past years when we might have reviewed the 3Ts.

First and foremost, we now have **more unencumbered time,** time to plan, to think things through, and perhaps to consider something new. The kids are gone. The demands of our career are behind us. We have flexibility and some room to maneuver that we probably didn't have the last time we thought about these things. Time, our most precious gift, has not increased, but our unallocated time has increased. Now we are unscripted, so how we decide to use the time we have is the most important decision we will make. Now is the opportunity to use it effectively to chart a new course, to rewire and redirect our daily activities to something that will be productive and satisfying.

Second, this time around, we have expanded **talents and skills that are tried and tested**. We know where we are productive and where we don't have much to offer. We have a lifetime of practicing what we are good at, after years of applying our talent and skills to the challenges of everyday life. In addition, we know what is satisfying – what we enjoy doing. That means we are in a stronger position to chart a new course because whatever we choose to do – however we plan to allocate our time – must center on activities that are both productive and satisfying.

Third, this time around, we have **added treasure,** more than we had when we started our career and probably more than we had at mid-life. Our net worth is likely larger. Though our income has declined if we are in our post-career years, so too have our expenses. With fewer domestic responsibilities and lower commuting, clothing and other costs associated with career work, we should have more control over our expenses.

But money is not the only measure of treasure. We also have a reputation that reflects our character, knowledge, reliability, integrity, and other virtues – and our capacity to perform. We have a larger network of friends and colleagues who can serve as resources for all kinds of purposes – companionship and collaboration, aid and comfort, advice and counsel – as we chart a new course for later life. And perhaps most importantly, we enjoy a larger reservoir of love – those we have loved and those who have loved us. Just as time is precious because once spent it is gone forever, love is precious because it is one of the few things that grows by giving, resulting in relationships that can be a source of strength, inspiration, solace, and even guidance, helping to keep us on course.

Also, because of these assets, it is more likely that we can take advantage of serendipity – the unexpected, the chance meeting or phone call, or something we see in our peripheral vision – provided we keep our eyes open. If we are alert and put our hand up as opportunities appear on the radar, we will find that good things often happen. So **there is a large role for serendipity** if we take a playful approach to scripting our post-career years. Writing the script for our post-career years need not be, and probably won't be. as literal and rational as we have described here. Still, the process of ending the old, taking time to think things through, and launching the new life by rebooting will be the same, whether it is explicit or not. So why not make it explicit?

Our time-out concludes when we are prepared to reboot. A reboot happens when we complete the script for our post-career life. Like new software for our computer, the new post-career script may involve some new programs and new applications, perhaps, for example, switching from full-time to part-time work, switching from paid work to volunteer work, or taking up disciplined enrichment work to learn a new skill. We may take up Samaritan work, taking care of ailing parents, or child care to help our kids adjust to a growing family in a two wage-earner environment. Still others will want to patch things up, do some repairs, make up for lost time in some area, or prepare for an altogether new life. Whatever the script, when we are comfortable with our new course, we press the reset button, we reboot, and get on with our new post-career life.

CHAPTER 15
TOOLS FOR A TIME-OUT

"Many – far too many – aspects of life...lie in the lumber-room among dusty memories; but sometimes, too, there are glowing coals under gray ashes."
– Carl Jung[237]

"It's not so much that we're afraid of change or so in love with the old ways, but it's the place in between that we fear. It's like being between trapezes. It's Linus when his blanket is in the dryer. There's nothing to hold on to."
– Marilyn Ferguson[238]

Psychologist David Guttmann tells us that **later life is a time when we begin to "run out of excuses."** This leads to a greater willingness to be frank and honest with ourselves, less prone to escape to illusions, and more accepting "without mercy" of our faults and shortcomings – a virtue he calls "spiritual freedom." If that is true, and I think it is, we can accomplish a lot, working on our own, in a self-directed time-out.[239] The key, of course, is to have an effective time-out – one that is thorough, honest, interactive, and concrete.

Effectiveness is best served by making sure your time-out is not an isolated activity. Even a self-directed time-out should involve others, people who know you well, to serve as mentors or accountability partners who can tell you the truth and give you honest feedback. Despite our growing spiritual freedom, we may still have blinders and need some help, at least with our peripheral vision. The **pool of potential accountability partners** might include family members, long-standing friends, or former colleagues who know you, whom you trust, and who will have your best interests at heart.[240]

There are also many good do-it-yourself tools to guide the self-assessment phase of your time-out. Here are four:

1. The autobiography. Nothing is more satisfying, or demanding, than writing. It requires focus, discipline, a schedule, and constant attention to what you want to say and how to say it. A writing agenda has a way of focusing the mind 24 hours a day. Writing makes you a keen observer of the world around you. Writing your own life story, the autobiography, also makes you a keen observer of your own life. Hence the autobiography can be used in a time-out to guide a self-assessment and serve as an agenda for discussion with your partner

A TIME-OUT FOR LATER LIFE

In later life, we are better equipped by our gifts, temperament, and experience to take a time-out to assess what's involved in a life that matters.

Of all our gifts – time, talent, and treasure – time is our most precious gift. Time is the most prized because it is the only gift that cannot be replaced. Time, once spent, is gone forever, so how we decide to use our time is the most important decision we will make, especially since unallocated time is something most of us will have in more abundance in our post-career life,

Our treasure includes money but also other assets, such as gifts of the intellect, e.g., wisdom, understanding, knowledge, and counsel; and gifts of the spirit, such as courage, fortitude, and piety. Treasure also includes our temperament, which at this stage of our life usually leaves us more reflective, more patient. That means we can take our time with our time-out. Let it stretch out, if need be. Seek out the views of others. Read. Think. Do mind sports. Take the time to listen and engage.

Treasure also encompasses experience, which includes a lifetime of exposure to learning from science, poetry, history, religion, politics; interacting with others in the home, the workplace, and in larger communities and institutions; and dealing with the world and its challenges. That's why we become wiser as we get older, provided we are even the slightest bit reflective about our life experiences. As St. Augustine said, "I come to know by doing."

Thus as we age and reflect on our experience we get more insight into our calling, that is, where we are productive (or fruitful) and what we find satisfying or fulfilling. We often find it on the job, in the work that we do. We also find it as we engage in family life, hobbies, or volunteer work.

The following story is a personal experience from my own family.

It was late one Friday evening. I had just returned from a week-long business trip. I was going through the mail from the previous week and found a FedEx from my uncle Walt. Walter Copper is the brother of my mother. He is now 86 years old. He was a B-24 pilot in World War II, a member of what Tom Brokaw called "the greatest generation." After the war, he and his wife, Barbara, raised a family and were actively involved in the lives of their kids and in the larger community.

When I opened the FedEx, I found 108 double-spaced pages of Uncle Walt's completed autobiography. In the foreword, he said he wrote it for his kids and grandkids, so they could know the history of their family, how their grandparents had experienced the Great Depression and World War II and then reignited their lives after the war was over. The first few pages grabbed my attention, and I read it at one sitting, finishing around 4:30 a.m.! It may not have been great literature, but it was a great read and a wonderful story of faith, true grit, optimism, merit, a strong work ethic, and most of all, love – love of family, community, and country. Uncle Walt's story is a personal treasure, and I know it will be a treasured legacy of our family for generations to come. In talking with my uncle after reading his *magnum opus,* it was clear that he found writing the autobiography both therapeutic and energizing and that it helped to provide a baseline for thinking through how he and his wife would spend the remaining years of their life.

By the way, as I was writing this section, I called Uncle Walt to tell him I would like to write about my experience with his autobiography. He approved, but during the course of our conversation, he told me that he was rewriting parts of his story, quickly assuring me that he wasn't changing anything, just "adding some details." I told him, "Uncle Walt, this is your story and you can tell it any way you want; it's your life and you can interpret it any way you want. That's what is great about the autobiography." If you don't interpret your story, someone else will.

There are many ways to approach your autobiography. [241] You may decide that your life story is best summed up by:
- **a theme**, e.g., the triumphant individual, rags-to-riches, your struggle, land of opportunity, etc. – think of the up-by-the-bootstraps theme that runs through American biography, from Abraham Lincoln's log cabin to the man from Hope we know as Bill Clinton;[242]
- **lessons learned**, an interesting approach used by Bill Gates' father in his recent autobiography, *Showing Up for a Life,*[243] or by St. Augustine in his *Confessions;*
- **a single event**, e.g., death of a parent, winning a prize,

getting married, birth of a child, losing an election, a road not taken, a major milestone – think of *Airborne: A Sentimental Journey*, by conservative icon William F. Buckley, a book based on the daily log of his month-long cruise across the Atlantic on his sailboat *Cyrano*, an event he uses to reflect on previous sailing experiences as far back as age 13 and to consider his success as a seaman and father;[244]

- **a single driver**, e.g., determination, fear of failure, desire to raise a family, to do good, or to make money – think of the 1987 screen classic, *Wall Street*, directed by Oliver Stone and starring Michael Douglas as Gordon Gekko, who made "greed is good" one of the memorable phrases of contemporary films;

- **a single characteristic**, e.g., a disability, a love of the outdoors, an aptitude for mathematics, a love of history – think of the 2001 Academy Award winning film, *A Beautiful Mind*, about mathematics prodigy John Nash, who overcame years of suffering with schizophrenia to win the Nobel Prize or *The King's Speech*, which is also an Academy Award-winning film, about King George VI's life-long struggle with stammering and his quest to find his voice...or read *Finding My Voice* (1999) by NPR talk show host Diane Rehm and how she continues to thrive with her nationally syndicated The Diane Rehm Show despite her on-going struggle with chronic spasmodic dysphonia – a neurological disorder that attacks the voice.

- **a single day**, e.g., the day you visited the Johnson Space Center, the day a teacher applauded your performance in math or English class, the day you lost your job, or like Henri Nouwen's life-changing experience the day he viewed Rembrandt's *The Prodigal* Son.[245]

Or, you may decide to tell it the old-fashioned way, chronologically from the beginning (when and where you were born, your upbringing, key events in your life) to the present.

There are all kinds of ways to go about telling your story, and you will be surprised how many among your family and friends will be interested in reading it. More importantly, you will be encouraged by how the exercise will help you clarify your own thinking, clearing the cobwebs from your mind as you set about charting a course for your post-career years.

LIFE AND STORY-TELLING[323]

Author, educator, and storyteller Norma Livo says, "The ability to tell stories – by ancient peoples as well as today's suburbanites – is the only art that exists in all human cultures. It is through stories that we experience our lives. The ability to tell a story is what sets people apart from all the other creatures of the Earth. It may be the one element that defines us as humans."

Writer Muriel Rukeyser takes it a step further. "The universe," she says, "is made of stories, not atoms," a view that seems to be supported by the enduring popularity of Aesop's fables or the fairy tales by Hans Christian Andersen or by the sales of anthologies of virtues by Bill Bennett or of Christmas stories by Joe Wheeler.

Regent University President Terry Lindvall, now retired, has said that the next century will be shaped by the people who can tell the best stories. And for good reason: stories, not just facts and data, are what move people, organizations, and nations to bigger and better things.

Good stories inspire. They convey knowledge. They create heroes and role models. They instill values. According to Livo, "Stories can be used to build self-confidence and persistence, to impart values and hopes, to demonstrate follies and triumphs, and to develop an optimistic outlook on life and show the listener or the reader that he or she is not the only one who ever experienced problems."

Thanksgiving dinner is a great time to tell stories, especially family yarns that focus on real people doing real deeds. Adults need to work at telling stories, to make sure they have clear story lines and crisp punch lines. Youngsters need to hear well-told stories because that's how they learn about good and bad – including shame and stigma and respect and reverence. It's an important way of describing behavior that we are in danger of losing in our "anything goes" culture.

In our family, we typically ask each person at the table to describe his or her favorite Thanksgiving or the one they remember the most. Sometimes we tell a story from history – like the Pilgrims' first Thanksgiving.

Danish futurist Rolf Jensen says, "In today's information society, we prize those who can skillfully manipulate data...in tomorrow's society, we will most generously reward those who can tell stories." Tomorrow is already here.

2. The auto-obituary. It may sound dark, but it shouldn't. Writing your own obituary can be an uplifting exercise and should be motivating.[246] It's a good exercise to undertake when you are 40, 50, or 60 – and certainly whenever you take your time-out. It will force you to examine what kind of life you have lived, what you have done, and how you want to be remembered.

The obit exercise also helps you to identify what remains to be done so that another will be able to write the obit you want when that time comes. Consider the obit of a guy named Jack Balmer of Vancouver, British Columbia, who wrote his own obituary for the *Vancouver Sun*:[247]

> As this is my auto-obituary, I'd like to write it in my own fashion! I was born in Vancouver on All Saints Day, 1931. Apart from practicing dentistry for 30 years, I have also at one time or another been fairly adept as a skier, private pilot, race car driver, vintner, mechanic, model builder, carpenter, photographer, plumber, scuba diver, writer, boat builder, Olympic team member (coach for a bronze medal), and a Canadian Coast Guard Auxiliary member. Since I've had a ball in life, with no regrets and nothing left still undone, and since our world seems to be quickly deteriorating, it's a good time for me to cash in. Goodbye, and good luck!

Jack's obit sounds like he led a life that made a difference, in several different settings, and it sounds like he led a full and satisfying life where he loved the adventure and loved the people with whom he worked and played – and was loved in return by others. It leaves a lot unsaid that I would like to know about, but it is his life in his words.

3. **Self-assessment exercises.** Some will approach their post-career later life unsure about what they want to do with the rest of their life. They may have a feeling that they want to do something new, something different, but are not quite sure what their cup of tea might be. That's where paper-and-pencil exercises can come in handy. Aptitude and other kinds of exercises help you assess what kind of work would fit with your gifts and would therefore make you productive and satisfied in later life.

These self-administered tests can help you discover your gifts. You might be surprised that you have developed new functional and transferable skills after 30 or 40 years of work, talents and skills that you now take for granted but have developed over time to change your gift profile dramatically and substantially.

Self-administered assessments can also help you to:
- Profile your later-life interests.
- Define a post-career mission for your later life.
- Evaluate the value of the career paths you have taken.
- Identify your later-life gifts, especially talents, skills, and treasures.
- Find new and reaffirm old purposes to guide your post-career later life.
- Chart a new course for later life, extending the old or trying something new.
- Prepare pros and cons of different working situations and which ones you prefer now, e.g., paid work or in-kind, volunteer, Samaritan, or enrichment work.
- Define your preferred working conditions, e.g., individual performer versus team member, large or small organization, start-up versus established organization, etc.
- Identify where and how you want to live in your post-career life.
- Identify the virtues and values that give meaning to your life.

There are many sources for these kinds of assessments. However, the most immediately accessible and practical collection of self-administered exercises with the best guidelines is an old favorite, *What Color is Your Parachute?*, especially the 2010 edition and the accompanying *Workbook*.[248]

Other excellent one-stop sources for self-assessment are *My Next Phase: The Personality-Based Guide to Your Best Retirement* and *Live Your Calling: A Practical Guide to Finding and Fulfilling Your Mission in Life,* especially the section entitled, "Creating Your Life Calling Map."[249]

There are also many online exercises you can consult to help you through your self-assessment. A good example is the Values in Action approach, called VIA Classification of Strengths. which can be used to identify your retirement strengths. The VIA can be found at www.viastrengths.org[250] These and other key sources for self-assessment are listed in the *Bibliographic Note*, found in Appendix B.

THE LIFE PORTFOLIO

There are many ways to approach your time-out assessment. One of the most powerful is the life portfolio, a comprehensive and holistic approach to assessing what is important in your life and how you should set priorities for your future. Invented by David Corbett, the life portfolio is an integrated approach to a process of self-discovery. Corbett describes the life portfolio as a framework for renewal:

"Your portfolio represents your work, your interest, what you have done... [and] can help make the most out of all of life...It is something portable, something you carry with you. The portfolio represents the whole. It [is] an expression of who you are. As work and life change, we take some elements out and put some elements in, which is just what we do when we reallocate or rebalance our investment portfolios...there is a portfolio perspective or mind-set that we may enter into at any age. It's a lifelong way of looking at your [work] integrated into the rest of your life...It speaks to what people are doing with their lives, how they are living and what they value – not their age or stage of life...it expands into a mindset that is ageless, in the broader sense of figuring out what really matters in life."

Corbett advises people to use what we call a time-out to look at five different ways they can invest their time and energy. These are:

1. Work – includes vocational or professional pursuits; the production of income;

2. Service – includes giving back through humanitarian or community engagement;

3. Personal growth – includes on-going learning and continuing education, self-development, intellectual stimulation, spiritual growth;

4. Relationships – includes cultivating connections to family and friends; and

5. Avocations – includes recreation, hobbies, pastimes.

Corbett's life portfolio includes an inventory of what he calls our internal drivers and external realities:

• Internal drivers include an assessment of your passions, energy, purpose, calling, skills, experience, credentials, wisdom, values, motivations, and legacy.

• External realities include financial, health and well-being, care-giving, preferences of your spouse or partner, and location.

You can prepare a Life Portfolio on your own by consulting David Corbett's *Portfolio Life: The New Path to Work, Purpose, and Passion after 50*. (San Francisco: Jossey-Bass, 2007) or by enrolling in a Life Portfolio program, provided by David Corbett and his colleagues at New Directions.

4. **The life portfolio.** Another approach to self-assessment is crafting a personal profile that is detailed and comprehensive, including purpose and calling as well as other concerns that need to be addressed in later life. The best I've seen is David Corbett's life portfolio concept.[251] The life portfolio is a comprehensive and holistic approach to assessing what is important in your life and how you should set priorities for your future. Corbett describes a life portfolio as a "framework for renewal" and an "expression of who you are," including your work, interests, and achievements. The life portfolio examines five ways to spend your time, including work, service, personal growth, relationships, and avocations.

CHAPTER 16
TIME-OUT TO BE

"First say to yourself what you would be and then do what you have to do."
– Epictetus

"There is an eagle in me that wants to soar, and there is a hippopotamus in me that wants to wallow in the mud."
– Carl Sandburg

"To be, or not to be, that is the question:
Whether 'tis nobler in the mind to suffer
The slings and arrows of outrageous fortune,
Or to take arms against a sea of troubles
And by opposing end them. To die – to sleep,
No more; and by a sleep to say we end
The heart-ache and the thousand natural shocks
That flesh is heir to: 'tis a consummation
Devoutly to be wish'd."
– Shakespeare, Hamlet, Act III, sc. i

Most of us will remember Shakespeare's most recognizable line: "To be, or not to be, that is the question..." These are the words of the indecisive and frustrated Hamlet as he thinks through whether the sting of death is preferable to the burdens of life. But when he looks at life, he sees it not in terms of who he is but only in terms of the consequences of living, e.g., slings and arrows, sea of troubles, natural shocks, and heartache. Focusing on the consequences only, Hamlet leaves unanswered the question of what it is to be.

So, to paraphrase Hamlet, the question is "What should we be?" As we enter our post-career years, we have a great opportunity to review what we have become and what we want to be in the years we have left.

- **For the secular person**, the answer will probably begin with being a good person, a faithful partner, a good citizen, a good provider, or other descriptions of being.

- **For the spiritual person**, the answer will begin with being a child of God, or a good and faithful servant of the Creator, or whatever or whomever we view as transcendent.

Whatever our worldview, later life is a time when we need to revisit what we want to be, something we may not have done since our late teens or early twenties.

One of the most interesting and challenging exercises in thinking through what we want to be is the **Be-Do-Have calculus**. Be-Do-Have is based on the work of the influential psychologist Eric Fromm, especially his book called *To Have or To Be?*[252] It is also reflected in the work of Henri Nouwen, noted in Chapter 5, where he reminds us that people falsely claim, "You are what you do (lawyer, mother, CEO, teacher, care-giver, scientist, unskilled laborer)...You are what you have (wealth, education, power, popularity, handicap, nothing)...You are what others think of you (kind, mean, saintly, loving, stupid)..." Instead, Nouwen, the theologian, declares that "We are not what we do. We are not what we have. We are not what others think of us...[we are the] child of a loving Creator."[253]

Some will be more comfortable in the corner of a secular psychologist such as Fromm. Others will feel more at home with a person of faith, such as the theologian Nouwen. Regardless of where we are most comfortable, most will find the Be-Do-Have calculus to be a powerful tool to discipline our thinking and planning for the future, in part because it forces us to **remember that it all begins with *being***. The idea goes something like this:

> If you can imagine what you want to be, then you'll be *inspired* to do what your being requires (or allows) you to do, and you will be *deterred* from doing things that are inconsistent with the ideals and requirements of your being. For example, a moral being, like any human being, is *able* to lie, cheat, and steal – but will strive not to. When your day-to-day activities reflect your being - i.e., when you harness your doing by the requirements of your being – your behavior is more likely to be aligned with and restrained by who you are.

But when we put our *haves* first, that's when we go off the tracks. There are at least two reasons. First, once you set your course by what you want to have – money, power, influence, fame, glory, lovers, honors, celebrity, space to live in, luxury cars, and the like –

you find that you can never have enough. You always want more, bigger, better, higher, newer, prettier, faster, or flashier.

Second, wanting to have something (say, wealth or fame or a job) will not discipline what you do. Ask the Enron guys who are now in jail. The lesson: Each of us is capable of doing all kinds of things, and the doing may well result in having wealth or success. But our doing may also cause broken friendships or families, or even land us in jail. That's why **we need a way to discipline what we do**, and that requires us to drive (and limit) our doing by who we are and what we want to be, not by what we want to have.

Think back to your experience with your own children when they were youngsters. At an early stage, youngsters start role-playing. They see themselves as a cowboy, princess, firefighter, astronaut, pirate, doctor, or nurse. They have an image of who they want to be. After deciding who they will be, they start acting out (i.e., doing) what the cowboy or princess would do – talking tough, arresting the bad guys, or dancing majestically around the room. If the role-playing continues over time, and it often does, sometimes for years, they will eventually want to have cowboy boots or a "diamond-studded" tiara and slippers.

Be-Do-Have, even with the youngster, starts with *being*. That seems to be the way we are wired in the womb. What little kids do naturally we should all do as we grow up. But as we grow up, our thinking often gets distorted and we get cross-wired. We learn from parents and the larger culture to take a different approach that puts doing or having first, e.g., Do-Have-Be, or Have-Do-Be. For example, we don't typically ask people, "Who are you, what's your story?" Instead, we ask them, "What do you do?" or "How many kids do you have?"

Think about this one. We often advise our kids: "If you work hard in school (do), you can get a good job (have), have success and become a civic leader (be). It continues into our later life, for example, "If we could have a townhouse at The Villages, we could play golf, take daily walks twelve months out of the year, and enjoy the company of other retirees (do); then we would surely be happy."

In fact, the kids get it right and the adults get it backwards. Our challenge is first to decide what we want to be, and everything else flows from that.

There are many ways to think about what we want to be in our post-career years. Consider, for example:

- a faithful follower
- a loving husband or wife
- a nurturing father
- a devoted mother
- an attentive grandparent
- a good provider
- a home-based business worker
- a volunteer
- an attentive son or daughter to aging parents
- a good neighbor

There are many other ways to describe what we want to be in our post-career years. Examples:

- happy
- contented
- a teacher
- a mentor/coach
- a counselor
- a performer
- a caretaker
- a troubleshooter
- a sports fan
- compassionate
- a good golfer
- grateful
- a runner
- healthy
- skinny
- a former smoker

These are but a few of the ways to describe what we want to be, and most of us will want to be more than one thing in our post-career years. However **most of us will have a hierarchy for what we want to be, because we consider some of our roles more important than others**. For example, if you are part of a faith tradition, then you will first and foremost want to be a faithful follower. In fact, author and social observer Os Guinness makes a distinction between what he calls our primary calling (to be a faithful follower) and our secondary callings (the roles we play as a worker, partner, or neighbor).

Even those who do not buy into a faith tradition will typically give a higher priority to some roles, e.g., family stewardship, and will let those trump other things they want to be, such as a sports fan or volunteer.

Next, we need to **decide what we need to do** (and can do) to be what we want to be.

- If we want to be a faithful follower, then we need to follow the precepts of a religion, spiritual worldview, or spiritual leader, or guru.
- If we want to be a good golfer, we need to practice every day, or at least three days a week.
- If we want to be a nurturing grandfather, then we need to spend time with our grandkids, teaching, telling stories, challenging, encouraging, caretaking.
- If we want to be compassionate, then we need to share in the suffering of others, by giving food to the hungry, clothing to the naked, sheltering the homeless, and visiting those in jail, to name a few things we can do.[254]
- If we want to be financially secure, then we must effectively manage our cash flow, make prudent investments, perhaps do some paid work, and/or practice frugality in our spending.

Finally, just as our being shapes and constrains what we do, **what we do will also shape what we have**. For example:

- If we want to be a faithful follower, adhering to the precepts of a religious or spiritual worldview, then we are more likely to have the peace, joy, and hope that comes with believing in that which we cannot see.
- If we want to be a good golfer and practice several times a week (do), then we are more likely (not guaranteed, but more likely) to have the joy and satisfaction that comes with self-improvement, increased competitiveness, and personal achievement.
- If we want to be a nurturing grandfather and we are attentive to (doing) the needs of our grandkids, then we are more likely (not guaranteed, but more likely) to have loving and self-confident grandchildren.
- If we want to be compassionate and visit (do) those in jail, we are more likely (not guaranteed, but more likely) to have

humility.

- If we want to be financially secure and if we do the right things, such as secure good financial advice, invest prudently, engage in paid work of some kind, and carefully control our spending, then we are more likely (not guaranteed, but more likely) to have financial peace of mind.

You get the picture. However, if we approach Be-Do-Have out of sequence, we risk becoming what one writer has called *"human doings,"* always busy, always occupied, always on the go with no time to lose. The result: Our being reflects busyness or perhaps even workaholism. Or we become *"human havings,"* obsessed by insatiable desires to have faster or bigger cars, a larger home, longer holidays, and other status symbols. The result: Our being reflects materialism and consumerism, even though we know deep down that we will never have enough. **Only when we begin with what we want to be, do we have the best chance of becoming a full human being**, where we let who we are both drive *and limit* what we do and what we seek to have.[255]

So, one of the most practical things we can do in a self-directed time-out is to complete a proper Be-Do-Have exercise. That requires us to (1) identify what we want to be. That means we need to think about the roles we want to play in our post-career years, to recall aspirations we've had and people we've admired as role models.[256] The important thing is to be who we are or to know (or discover) who we want to be.

When we know our life's purpose, what matters to us, and what gives our life meaning, then (2) we list the doing activities we would undertake to give life to that kind of person – a sort of to-do list where we weigh our gifts and how they can best be applied, and understand our strengths and weaknesses.

Finally, (3) we list the things or situations we want or need to have. An example of a Be-Do-Have list is shown in Figure 4.

In these past two chapters, we have covered five different strategies to help you have a productive time-out. Even more strategies and resources are available to stimulate your thinking and enrich your time-out. We are not going to reproduce them here, though links to many are found in the *Bibliographic Note* in Appendix B.

Figure 4: Be-Do-Have: A Secular, Middle Class Example

Be	Do	Have
A faithful partner	Honor, respect, and love spouse; Be there, care, and share, esp. more time in joint activities; be patient; listen, assist with activities of daily living.	Happy home life Affection, respect Joy, contentment Better health
A good provider	Seek professional help to manage savings more effectively; reduce costs, manage spending; buy long-term care insurance; secure part-time paid work to minimize draw on nest egg.	A secure net worth More money, choices Peace of mind New car Legacy for kids
A loving parent, involved with my family	Prepare a family tree for the kids and grandkids; create/maintain family traditions; participate in lives of grandkids; encourage/mentor grandkids.	A strong family life Impact on grandkids The blessing of leaving a legacy
A fit person	Swim every day; join water aerobics group; maintain weight; eat properly; do brain sports; work; get annual check-up; follow physician's advice.	Independence Ability to help others Longer, better life Happiness
A giving person	Assist young business owners as a volunteer advisor; give generously to church, nonprofit charities; tell people (e.g., a soldier, your barber) you appreciate what they do; do volunteer work.	Community spirit Giving back Satisfaction from doing what's right and helping others
An engaged citizen, involved in my community	Secure part-time paid work; perform community service through Rotary and the neighborhood association; take classes on using computer; get involved in theater; join history book club.	Obligations to others Accountable to others Servant heart Networks beyond family, neighborhood

CHAPTER 17
A COMPASS FOR THE POST-CAREER YEARS

"...we need a whole new scenario for ...the second half of life...Of one thing there is little doubt: if we hang on to old expectations, we are more likely than not to live down to them."
– William A. Sadler[257]

"Your successes and happiness are forgiven you only if you generously consent to share them."
– Albert Camus, The Fall

"The things I am most proud of, I've done in the past five years."
– Armand Hammer, said when past 90[258]

"Here lies a miser who cared for himself,
He cared for nothing but gathering wealth.
Now where he is and how he fares
Nobody knows and nobody cares."
– Old English gravestone[259]

"Two roads diverged in a wood, and I –
I took the one less traveled by,
And that has made all the difference."
– Robert Frost

Let's review the bidding. In a nutshell, we can summarize as follows:

1. **Later life begins at age 50**. That is a good time to begin to think about the post-career years of your life – what you want to be, what you are going to do, and how you are going to manage your time.

2. **Most of us, going by the averages, retire from our career in our early sixties,** which means that our post-career life will, for most

of us, be measured in decades. We need to use that time wisely, to experience a life of meaning, to navigate a life that matters.

3. **When we retire, most of us are healthy and at the top of our game,** still able to contribute to our family, our community, and the larger society. That's why it makes sense, both practically and morally, to continue to use our major gifts to help others and to make the world a better place. We are able to do it, and we should do it.

4. **Of our three major gifts – time, talent, and treasure – time is the most important.** Time is the only resource we have that cannot be replaced. Time, once spent, is gone forever. So our major challenge is to decide how to manage our time so it can be used to bring meaning to our post-career years.

5. **Of all of the drivers of successful aging,** e.g., physical fitness, mental sharpness, good nutrition, financial well-being, and social engagement. **the most important is social engagement** or active participation with other people in purposeful activity. Active engagement fosters mental sharpness, exposes one to good practices around nutrition and physical fitness, and if it is associated with paid work, can lead to improved financial well-being.

6. **Work is a sure path to social engagement when we transition to our post-career life.** There are other paths to engagement – hobbies, games, crafts, sports, and the arts, for example – but work has many advantages. Work comes in many flavors, both full time and part time, and work provides many paths to achieve active engagement with others: work for pay, in-kind work, volunteering, Samaritan work, and enrichment work. Work gives us all an opportunity to continue to contribute to the well-being of others and to the betterment of society.

7. **Transitions require a time-out,** unencumbered time to think, reflect, dream, and plan. We use the time-out to leave our old life behind and then refocus on our post-career years, that is, write a script for our new post-career life and then reboot.

8. **We should take a two-chapter approach when rebooting to our post-career life**, beginning with Script 1.0, which keeps us on the clock, working in some capacity that has obligations and accountabilities; and depending on circumstances (e.g., health, well-being) or personal preferences, ending with Script

2.0, which takes us off the clock into a life of leisure or a life focused on the activities of daily living.

9. **A script can have many versions or releases**. As we move through different phases of our post-career years we will make revisions in our script – Script 1.0 morphs into Release 1.1, 1.2, etc. Revisions will be prompted by discovering that some things we planned just didn't work out. New releases will also be prompted by discovering unanticipated opportunities that take us down a new path. The different releases will reflect the different combinations of work, leisure, and activities of daily living by which we manage our time.

10. **We should remain on the clock as long as possible** in our post-career years, maintaining obligations and accountabilities to others. The alternative is to go off the clock, where we are only accountable to ourselves. Going off the clock can be voluntary, motivated by a desire for leisure or a need to off-load obligations – or it can be involuntary, occasioned by disability or frailty.

11. **We should clarify the purposes that will drive our post-career life.** When we take a time-out for post-career planning and to reboot for engagement in our post-career years, we need to ask: Engagement for what? Longevity for what? Successful aging for what?

12. **Different worldviews and belief systems, including the spiritual, New Age, and secular, share common perspectives about life's purpose,** namely, that our purpose in life is (a) to help others, (b) to repair the world or make it a better place (or at least that part of the world, no matter how small, that we can influence), and to do it in a way that is (c) fruitful and productive for our family or the community and (d) satisfying to us. Whatever our worldview, we should aim to live a life of meaning by helping others and improving the world and by engaging in a post-career life that is productive and satisfying, as summarized in the graphic below.

So as we approach our post-career years, we should seek a clear direction and maintain our peripheral vision to catch serendipitous opportunities. Throughout the process, we need to focus on who we want to be, what we want to do, and what we want to have.

As we pick our destination and select our waypoints, we have **aids to navigation** that include a *behavioral compass* for successful aging (which points to continued social engagement) and a *moral compass* (which points to helping others and improving the world).[260] It is important to spotlight that both the behavioral compass and the moral compass will point in the same direction – namely, to remain on the clock with obligations and accountabilities to others for as long as possible.

In keeping with the compass analogy, we should continue to work in some capacity because **work is true North**, the destination suggested both by the moral compass (using our gifts to benefit others) and the behavioral compass for successful aging (social engagement).

Our message for now is simple: When you retire from your career, take a time-out. Use your time-out to map a two-chapter, post-career life that includes a plan to go back to work in some capacity, from paid work and volunteering, to in-kind work, Samaritan work, or an enrichment commitment. Reasons:

Work is good for the soul; work was, after all, created for us to do, and work, as noted, is "love made visible."

Work is good at keeping you engaged in the world and involved with others – and that is important because social engagement is the key to successful aging.

Work allows you to help others and to make the world a better place, two important elements of leading a life that matters that are widely shared among those who otherwise hold different worldviews – including spiritual, New Age, and secular worldviews.

Work (if you work for pay) can also help fill your pocketbook so you can more easily take care of yourself and others.

Many will reboot to paid work because they have no choice. Many didn't save enough money and need to keep working to keep eating. Others saved and invested, but lost a good part of their nest egg in the dot-com bust in 2000 or later in the Great Recession beginning in 2008. But even if you must work for pay because you need income, you should return to paid work with the knowledge that work is in your best interest and, frankly, in the best interest of our society. There is always work that needs to be done.

Figure 5: Elements of a Life of Meaning

On the demand side, industry and commerce need talent badly, and even in bad times, when there is a lot of unemployment, later-life employees often look more attractive in the New Economy of knowledge workers than they did in the old muscle economy that valued time-and-motion performance over mental agility. In addition, of course, older workers are tried and tested, possess relevant know-how, and are usually more reliable and adaptable – all qualities that lead to greater productivity. That's why we are likely to see more flexible approaches by business and other employers to hiring – or re-hiring – those approaching their post-career years.

Business is sometimes slow to see social trends but is almost always fast in catching up. That's what is happening now. Hence, when you go to your employer, assuming you want to remain in your current career path or your current place of work (though perhaps in a different job), you can help move the dial in the direction of greater flexibility. As more later-life Americans remain on the job but perhaps in a different role – or to work part-time instead of full-time or work from home – business managers will respond. Why? Because competitive enterprises don't turn their back on tried-and-tested talent, business enterprises are always in the market for people who will make them more nimble, innovative and productive, even in a slow economy.

At the societal level, demographic trends are disturbing.[261] Between 2010 and 2030 the number of Americans age 65 or more will increase from 41 million to 71 million. This age wave will create even more financial pressure on a government already stressed by its own long-time mismanagement of the nation's wealth.[262] The huge unfunded promises that have been made to later-life Americans for Social Security and Medicare total more than $100 trillion in today's dollars.[263] This includes:

• Social Security promises totaling $17 trillion.

• Medicare Part A (hospital care) totaling $36 trillion

• Medicare Part B (medical visits) totaling $37 trillion

• Medicare Part D (prescription drugs) totaling $15 trillion

Result: It is just a matter of time until the official retirement age is extended to 70 or older...along with a reduction of benefits. As noted earlier, if the retirement age were indexed to longevity increases since 1935, today's retirement age would be 82. So, as the Social

Security retirement age is increased and benefits are reduced, there will be clear need for post-career later-life American to work longer. Though the government's failure to keep its promises will cause many to feel betrayed, the need to devote more time to work may be a blessing in disguise.

I am confident more Americans will come to the view that staying on the clock as long as possible is a good thing – and for many, it will be necessary. Most Americans, even if they aren't required to work for financial reasons, will remain on the clock as they come to understand that work improves their health, wealth, and moral well-being.

That's why we must retire the word, the idea, and practice of retirement. That's why we must continue to work, in some capacity, as long as we are physically and mentally able. Work is our calling. Working to help others and to make the world a better place is why we are here. Our work – our good deeds and the good things we create with our family and friends and provide for our community and our society – is an important part of our legacy.

In short, when we reboot **we need to write a two-chapter script for our post-career life**, making sure that work is part of our script and has a central place in our post-career life portfolio.

REFORMS TO ATTRACT LATER-LIFE EMPLOYEES

Employers increasingly recognize the need to attract and retain more qualified and experienced later-life employees. Large companies, especially, need to retain their older, more skilled and experienced employees, especially as the proportion of workers in the 25 to 44 age group declines. Older workers have the knowledge, skills, and temperament to do the jobs that have to be done, from the factory floor to the executive suite, something long-recognized by hospitals and retailers. Moreover, older employees provide institutional memory and mentoring and are a key element in knowledge management, particularly in large enterprises.

Later-life employees are especially valuable in small and mid-sized enterprises (SMEs) because of their reliability, skills, adaptability, and flexibility. For example, consider the public attention given to the practice of many McDonald's franchisees to hire later-life Americans because they provide good role models for proper workplace behavior and performance for young and often first-time job holders.

Many business organizations and business-oriented nonprofits are giving more attention to companies that innovate in the recruitment and retention of later-life Americans, including the AARP's Innovative Employer Awards, which celebrate employers that provide opportunities for long-term employees. AARP also designates Best Employers for Workers Over 50, which has recognized more than 130 cutting-edge companies "whose best practices and policies for addressing the issues of an aging workforce are roadmaps for the workplaces of tomorrow." [328]

Companies that want to be more attractive to later-life workers should consider policies and practices for boomers who often seek flexibility, connections, and opportunities for personal growth and to give something back.[329] Thus, age-friendly companies will give attention to:

- Recruiting practices, including working with senior centers and other later-life groups to recruit mature workers.
- Workplace culture, such as flexible scheduling, telecommuting, job-sharing, and phased-in retirement; caregiver support programs for sandwich-generation workers; and older workers as mentors and expert teachers.
- Lifelong learning opportunities, including financial planning, pre-retirement preparation seminars and workshops.
- Education and job-training opportunities, including computer skills and refresher courses for people who have been out of the workforce for a time.

- Alternative work options, such as employee benefits that support the health and financial security of employees.
- Workplace design, such as ergonomic work stations and facilities that take into account the needs of later-life individuals.
- Retiree relations, such as continued access to company stores and fitness centers, maintaining a data base of post-career employees who are interested in returning to work in some capacity, volunteer-based company museums and oral history projects.

CHAPTER 18
GETTING IT RIGHT

"Age is opportunity no less than youth itself."
– Henry Wadsworth Longfellow

"Be occupied with...things and issues that are of interest, importance, and concern to you. Remain passionately involved in them."
– Morrie Schwartz[264]

As I was digging out of the worst winter weather in the recent history of the Mid-Atlantic region, I spotted my energetic neighbor, Ray Van Horn, who is also retired and was also digging out. Ray is an active, upbeat, and curious age 71 – and pretty good at shoveling snow. He retired at age 65, more than five years ago. We talked a bit and decided to continue our conversation at breakfast the next morning at a local café called Grumps.

We met as planned and, after we ordered, I asked Ray how the "retirement thing" was working. "Pretty well," he said. "I can't complain."

I asked him because having been away in Australia for more than three years, I hadn't talked with him for a long time. But I remembered that before I left, he had been struggling to adjust to his post-career life. He confirmed that his transition had not been easy, but he was now through it and in good shape. Then he told me a really interesting story, including how he got back on track.

Ray was born in Ohio and raised in the Midwest, ending up in Wisconsin. He got interested in photography when he was a teenager. He was heading toward a career in photography, but when the time came to think about his postsecondary education, his father said, "You can't make a living taking pictures." Ray was a good son. He listened to his father, so he went to the Illinois Institute of Technology and became an engineer. After that, he went to work for BorgWarner and, after a while, won a slot in the management training program and eventually earned an MBA at the University of Chicago.

Ray had a good career in manufacturing, building on his engineering education, a career that included running the Canadian operations of a BorgWarner subsidiary. But Ray is a people person and found his strong suit was in technology sales and marketing. Ray ended up spending the last phase of his 40-year career selling industrial products to a variety of customers, but primarily to the government.

When Ray retired he was looking forward to fishing, playing golf, sailing, kayaking, and spending more time with Lynne, his wife of 47 years, his two grown children, and six grandchildren. But after a year or so, he was bored and restless with full-time leisure.

When he told me that, I asked, "How did you go about getting out of this retirement *cul-de-sac*? Did you do it on your own or what?" His reply was very interesting:

> I'm a trained engineer and spent my early years in product development, so I like systems, plans, lists. But I also had another perspective and skill-set that came from spending most of my career in sales, selling engineered products to enterprise and government customers.
>
> You learn a lot of important skills when you are a salesman – especially how to manage your time. It works like this. First, a salesman has to satisfy his customers. That means our mission is clear; it is a given; it's right up front; and we all know what it is and how progress will be measured [purpose]. Second, most salesmen I know have a route [a plan] every week: Dover AFB on Monday, Fort McNair on Tuesday, the Pentagon on Wednesday, etc. But that's all I had, just the route. After that, I had what we call an *open book*. That means every day I had to make choices about what I was going to do with each of the customers on my route, trying to anticipate what the customer would want to talk about or what I should talk about. Was I going to deal with a problem I knew the customer was having? Was I going to review a change in the customer's environment? Was I going to see the top guy or guys in the

trenches? Was I going to push a new or improved product? I had to fill my book every day by my own initiative, using my own judgment.

So, as I grew frustrated with my retirement, I sat down and thought things through. I simply used the strategies I learned over a lifetime of working. First, I took a breather [time-out] just to focus on how I was spending my post-career time compared to what I wanted to do. It didn't take long to realize that I wanted to focus on my family and use my experience to help others [purpose]. I wanted to give back to my family by spending more time with them and using my skills in photography to create a legacy of our growing up together. I also wanted to use my experience in business to come alongside and help younger business leaders. There were other things, but I had enough to create a roadmap or route [script] for each of the seven days of the week. That left seven days where I had to fill my book with activities consistent with how I wanted to spend my post-career years [a reboot].

Note the words in brackets above are the words used throughout this book to describe how we can reboot for retirement. Ray actually went through most of the steps we have discussed.

It is interesting as well to notice how Ray thought about his gifts of *time* (manage it to a purpose), *talent* (photography, ability to work with people, and business sales, marketing and management experience), and *treasure* (a collection of thousands of family pictures, a place to work at home, knowledge of government procurement, good health and lots of energy, and retirement income, giving him the freedom to choose his work).

The substance of Ray's reboot is even more interesting. Ray decided to devote part of his retirement to changing lanes. The first thing he did was to resurrect his first love, photography. He decided to devote at least one day a week to getting up to speed with the new digital photography technologies, learning how to use them, and installing them on his computer. He also had an opportunity to continue to do some consulting with his former employer. In short, Ray made a plan, and it looks like this:

Monday: Digitize several thousand family photos, assemble nine unique albums, one for each of the two kids, six grandkids, and one for home. He is also writing a family memoir laced with pics from his photo collection. He is taking courses and workshops at the Anne Arundel Community College on digital technology and software to keep up with new developments in digital photography. He also attends a workshop on writing memoirs at the Anne Arundel County senior center. The courses and workshops are often scheduled on other days of the week, but he considers them part of his "Monday mission."

Tuesday: Volunteer as an advisor for the Senior Corps of Retired Executives, a federal program known as SCORE, to provide technical and management assistance to small and mid-sized business companies. Ray has worked with more than 150 companies since retirement.

Wednesday: Provide fee-based consulting services to his previous employer, focused on technical and management assistance with government contracting work. Though he usually works a day a week at this, if there is no work, then he uses the day for his "Monday mission" or for golfing, sailing, kayaking, fishing, what he calls GSKF.

Thursday: GSKF, some other recreation activity. In bad weather, he uses the day for his "Monday mission" – i.e., home time for his photography project.

Friday: Day trips that sometimes extend into the weekend, home maintenance, special projects, work through the honey-do list, etc.

Saturday: Relax with friends, neighbors, and relatives.

Sunday: Church at Annapolis Presbyterian, relax with friends, neighbors, and relatives.

This is an "in general" schedule because Ray and his wife devote nearly 100 days (almost 14 weeks total) to visits with his immediate family, and during that time, he doesn't work at all. This includes 76 days a year to grandkids just up the road in Gaithersburg, Maryland (24 trips of two days) and for longer trips to Nashville, Tennessee (four trips of seven days). He also uses about 20 days a year for visits with his 95 year-old mother in Findlay, Ohio (four trips of five days each). He and his wife drive on most of these trips because they enjoy the time together and like having a car when they get to their destination.

That means his weekly schedule applies to about 38 weeks a year – since he is away the other 14. If we translate all of that into the five types of work we discussed in *Reboot!* Chapter 8, it would look like this:

Figure 6: Ray's Post-Career Script for the Week

Day	Activity Description	Reboot Activity Type
Monday	Photography work, family albums, memoir	Enrichment Work
Tuesday	Volunteer advisor for SCORE	Volunteer Work
Wednesday	Fee-based consulting	Paid Work
Thursday	Recreation: golf, sailing, kayaking, fishing	Leisure & Recreation
Friday	Home maintenance, special projects, day trips	Family & Friends
Saturday	Home time, neighbors, relatives	Family & Friends
Sunday	Church, home time, neighbors, relatives	Family & Friends

So, in a normal week, a week where he is not visiting out-of-town family, Ray spends about 50 percent of his time working (three to four days); about 35 percent of his time with family, friends, and neighbors (two to three days); and about 15 percent in leisure activities (one day), though many segments of time spent with family, friends, and neighbors also include leisure activities.

The conversation with Ray was intriguing to me for another reason. Though Ray and I didn't discuss this, as I listened to him describe his journey, I could see his way of thinking followed a Be-Do-Have approach – though he probably wouldn't describe it that way. For example, Ray wanted to be a photographer, reigniting an old dream from his teenage years. He moved from that to doing: taking courses at the community college to get up to speed on digital photography and then producing (doing) picture albums for each of the kids and grandkids. That doing allowed him to have a record of the family's good times. It shows the growth and development of the kids, and provides an agenda of pictures and stories to tell his grandkids and a family legacy that he and his wife can leave behind. He seemed to go through the same thought process in other areas as well, first thinking about what he wanted to be: photographer, faithful and engaged husband, loving and committed grandfather, engaged worker in several kinds of work, and an involved friend and neighbor. Then he moved to doing and having. Just the way it should be done.

During the course of our conversation, Ray said, as an aside, he thought **the discipline to say no is the most important discipline to develop in your post-career life**. That's one reason he made the weekly schedule (like the weekly route that guided his comings and goings when he was selling); it gave him an easy way to say no. If SCORE wants him to do something, he can say yes, provided it's on Tuesday. If the guys want him to go sailing, that can work for Ray, provided it's on Thursday, etc. Then he said, with a twinkle in his eye, "But you can be flexible to a point. You make the rules in the first place, so you can break the rules, and that's OK because you're retired."

As we finished our breakfast at Grumps, we also touched on how the spouse fits into this post-career thing. Grumps, the neighborhood eatery noted for its zany décor and wacky signs, had one that proclaimed: "When the queen is happy, there is peace in the palace." Ray pointed to the sign and said, "You can't forget the spouse in the book you are writing." Then he said, "It works both ways – I mean both the queen and the king have to be happy for the palace to be happy." We agreed on that. Indeed, everything we have talked about in these pages applies equally to men and women. Still, there are many issues unique to women, both the stay-at-home mom and the career woman that need to be addressed...and are in other places.[265]

EPILOGUE
GOING OFF THE CLOCK

"We are all happier in many ways when we are old than when we are young. The young sow wild oats. The old grow sage."
– Winston Churchill

"Over a lifetime, there should be a time to grow, time to work, and finally time to rest."
– Rowe and Kahn[266]

"There is a time for everything, and a season for every activity under heaven: a time to be born and a time to die; a time to plant and a time to uproot...a time to tear down and a time to build; a time to weep and a time to laugh... a time to search and a time to give up; a time to keep and a time to throw away...a time to be silent and a time to speak..."
– Ecclesiastes 3:1-8

I remember many years ago when I was part of a team working on a project in Mexico, I was required to learn some Spanish. I didn't learn as much as I should have, but I did learn to appreciate what my 11th grade Spanish teacher told me: If you are truly to appreciate another culture, you must know its language.

The truth of that observation came to me when I learned that the Spanish word for a business or doing business is *negocio*. The root word is *ocio*, which means idleness, spare time, leisure time, useless, to do nothing.

So what is business? A business is the negative or the opposite of doing nothing, which means to do something, to set up or talk business, to make a deal or trade, or employment. But literally *negocio* means not to do nothing. Does this imply that doing nothing is OK?[267]

There are many cultures in the world where doing nothing is taken more seriously than it is in America. In the US, we give doing nothing a name: we call it a vacation, and most of us work at it. In fact, I can't count the times my wife and I were happy that our vacation was over. On the other hand, North Americans do value the coffee break. I suppose that is a good example of doing nothing, just as the English, Australians, and other Commonwealth countries break for morning tea and again for afternoon tea.

But in other cultures, doing nothing has been a more central and honored part of everyday life. In Mexico, it is called *siesta*. A *siesta*, of course, is a short nap taken in the early afternoon, typically after lunch. This practice of relaxation, even sleep, has in the past included going home to spend quiet time with the family.[268]

Ocio – doing nothing – is what many people look forward to when their careers are over. Though it's my view that we should keep working as long as we are able, I am not altogether unsympathetic to the view that there is a time for doing nothing.

Ideally, we would go off the clock when we no longer want (or have lost the ability) to be accountable to others. When you go off the clock voluntarily, you no longer want to have obligations or remain on a schedule that requires you to perform on a regular basis. You want to quit your job. You want to give up your volunteer responsibilities. You want, or need, to reduce the pressures to perform, meet a schedule, be on time, and conform to a to-do list.

However, being off the clock doesn't necessarily mean you aren't engaged. But your engagement with others is entirely on your terms and for your satisfaction. That's why I call this kind of engagement off the clock.

Because I enjoy sailing, I read sailing magazines. I was moved when I came across an *"ocio* story" about novelist and Pulitzer Prize-winning poet Conrad Aiken in a 2009 issue of *Cruising World*. The writer, Webb Chiles, himself a sailor, tells it this way:

> Aiken and his wife used to take a pitcher of martinis and go sit near his parents' grave in a cemetery overlooking the harbor at Savannah, Georgia. One afternoon, he noticed a ship pass with the name *Cosmos Mariner*, which pleased him...[W]hen he checked the newspaper's shipping news he read this: "*Cosmos Mariner*: destination unknown", which pleased him even more.[269]

Chiles goes on to write:

> I found myself counting back to when I'd last sailed
> into Whangamumu [a small New Zealand harbor]. It
> must have been...fifteen years ago. [Now] at the age
> of 65, it seemed...unlikely that I'd be sailing in again
> 15 years from now. But then again, I might.[270]

> Cosmos mariners. Destinations unknown.

So, here we have an example of a writer and his subject, both of whom appear to appreciate the value of a life that is off the clock but still engaged. If we remember that successful aging is about living a good life – one that provides a sense of fulfillment – then both Aiken and Chiles are revealed as finishing well. If we look at this from a faith-based perspective, both are clearly experiencing and appreciating God's creation. Sometimes you give through work and deeds. Sometimes you take by experiencing creation or through personal growth. Each can contribute to successful aging, each can be undertaken on your own terms, and each can be achieved off the clock.

So, unless we die with our boots on (my preferred outcome), fully engaged and doing good work helping others and improving that part of the world we can touch, we will, at some point decide, or be required by circumstances, to go off the clock and move into Script 2.0.

When that happens, maybe it's because we are weary and need to wind down. Perhaps we are disabled. Maybe we are burned out. Maybe we are healthy but have simply reached the point where we have nothing left to give to the world of work and want to retire to doing nothing, doing nothing but enjoying life, giving to our family and friends, experiencing the world, and confronting the inevitable trials that come with the end of life. The Script 2.0 *ocio* life" will come to all of us who survive long enough, but when it happens, we should be thankful that we were blessed with the opportunity to work so long. Work is made for man...

ACKNOWLEDGMENTS

Reboot! is rooted in my personal experience. Writing this book has been on my mind for most of the past decade, beginning with my own failed retirement when I turned 60. Still, my views have been influenced by many sources. These include the writings of many dozens of scholars and commentators whose work is cited throughout; the insights of professionals in the aging community who gave me the benefit of their time and experience; the critiques of many friends and colleagues who reviewed drafts of *Reboot!*; the testimony of retirees and failed retirees who told me their stories and shared their life's lessons; and the views of my family, first and foremost my wife, Mary Sue, and our grown children, David, Katie, and Ben, who were always supportive and encouraging and whose continuing stream of comments were often stimulating and always useful. My experience with them as critics reflected well on their education in the social sciences, the law, and business and their perspective as recent entrants to a workforce that is increasingly skeptical that they will ever see income from a government-sponsored retirement program.

I am indebted to many friends and colleagues who provided rich and useful critiques of drafts of *Reboot!* – not the least Ned Brooks, who provided the first (and very agonizing) critique that led to an early reorganization of the material. Others providing useful comments included Bill Bass, Dan and Jackie Billingsley, Kent Briggs, Lynn Cooper, Jim Davis, Dan Martin, Robert Morrison, Rick O'Donnell, George Pendleton, Ken and Pam Prickett, Sam Sydney, Therese Waldkirch, and Denny and Dorothy Whitford – along with friends and colleagues in Australia, including Sandra Carter, Julia Foley, Michael Grealy, Samantha (Sam) Kennedy, Craig Perrett, Janie Gough, and Cassandra Scott. Special thanks go to Imogen Zethoven, who was especially helpful with ideas for the closing chapters of *Reboot!* and Henry Ergas, who helped me understand the role of pension systems in industrial economies.

My thinking about the importance of working during the post-career years was sharpened by many discussions with civic leaders and leaders of business, government and the nonprofit sectors

– including Jeff Cole, Jeffrey Furniss, Henry Goldstein, Tom Kerr, Adm. Jack Kersh, Elizabeth Liechty, Robert Morrison, Daniel Moneypenny, John Mariotti, Pam Palumbo, Detlaf Rathmann, Lee Scott, Jonathan Steele, Jeff Sandefer, Sol Trujillo, Chad Watson, and JoLynne Whiting – and by physicians, psychologists, and other professionals in the health care community: Carol Betson, Martin (Chip) Doordan, Roger Doyel, Kate Morrison, Orlie Reid, Marshall Steele, Jack Wagoner, and Louise Weaver.

My effort to address religious and spiritual dimensions of success-ful aging from an inter-faith perspective were informed especially by the writings and sometimes competing views of George Barna, Os Guinness, Rabbi Harold Kushner, Stephen Prothero, Huston Smith, and Dallas Willard, and by discussions with and critiques by Dorothy Bass, John Bishop, Norm Brown, Dave Castle, Doug Coe, Lou Higgs, Ron Holden, Larry Kooi, Bob Moffitt, Gary Pielemeier; and in Australia, Rev. Donald Howard and Philip Jensen, Dean of the Sydney Cathedral.

I am especially grateful to those who allowed me to write about their lives – including Virginia Burgess (to whom this book is dedi-cated), Walter Copper, Ray Van Horn, Ed Fergus, John Kenny and those whose stories I have told but who have gone unnamed by mutual agreement.

I want to acknowledge the highly professional work of Kirby Tarzwell, Sabrina Ali and FriesenPress for their important contribution to the design, editing, and timely publication of *Reboot!* Similarly, I am indebted to Robert Dilenschneider of the Dilenschneider Group, Inc. in New York City and Richard Levick of Levick Strategic Communications in Washington, D.C. for their public relations ad-vice and counsel.

In addition, Jeff and Valerie Cochran of Exclamation Communications, Inc., Jonathan Oleisky and Colleen McKenna Media924 and Steve Case of Case Development, LLC were instrumental in helping me take full advantage of the Internet – especially an integrated strate-gy for linking my website **www.BooterNation.com** with Facebook, Twitter, LinkedIn, and other social media – to build a community around *Reboot!* I also benefited from discussions with Melissa Arnoff, Sean McNair, Chris Brooks and others at Levick Strategic

Communications, and with Rob Key and Paull Young at Converseon in New York about the use of the new digital media to spread ideas.

Two people deserve special thanks – my agent, Joe Tessitore, who advanced my project through the gauntlet of editors during 2010 and taught me a lot about the rapidly changing business of publishing books; and David Jamison who was a faithful and constructive partner in this project going back to 2004, when he began teasing my interest in later-life transitions with a weekly supply of newspaper and magazine articles about America's changing demographics, changing views of retirement, the looming crisis in Social Security and other age-related entitlements, and changing patterns of post-career life styles and the spiritual needs of later-life Americans – just as the ideas leading to *Reboot!* were beginning to take shape.

Finally, I want to thank Danny Leydorf for his invaluable research assistance, Brad Whitford and Valerie Cochran for their design and graphics skills, and Debbie Sherr for her help with word processing and assembly. Each played key roles at various stages in the completion of this project.

As much as I am indebted to these, and to others unmentioned, for their invaluable help and wise counsel along the way, I alone am responsible for any errors of fact or interpretation.

Phil Burgess
Annapolis, Maryland

ABOUT THE AUTHOR

Phil Burgess is an award-winning educator, businessman, and writer who has lectured world-wide – in the Americas, Europe, Australia and Asia, including Japan, China, India, Korea, and Vietnam. He has appeared on PBS, NPR, CNN, and CNBC, and his views have been reported in regional, national and international media – including *The Denver Post, The New York Times, Wall Street Journal, Sydney Morning Herald*, Tokyo's *Asahi Shimbun* and *Vital Speeches*. He wrote more than 350 weekly op-ed commentaries on America's political culture from 1990-2001. His commentaries in the Denver-based *Rocky Mountain News*, were nationally distributed to more than 140 newspapers by Scripps Howard News Service, and are available at www.annapolisinstitute.net.

Phil had three careers before becoming a booter – first as a professor at The Ohio State University, University of Colorado, and Colorado School of Mines, where he taught public policy, public management, and resource economics; second, as chief executive of non-profits and think tanks focused on public policy – including the Federation of Rocky Mountain States, Western Governors' Policy Office, Center for the New West, Western Coal Export Council, and National Academy of Public Administration; and third, as a senior executive at large-cap, media-communications companies: US West (now Qwest) and Telstra (Australia's telecommunications giant) where he was also a visiting professor at the business school of the Royal Melbourne Institute of Technology (RMIT).

The former Fulbright Scholar received his undergraduate degree from Knox College in Galesburg, Illinois and his Ph.D. from The American University in Washington, D.C. Phil is currently president of The Annapolis Institute and a senior fellow at the University of Southern California's Center for the Digital Future.

Phil and Mary Sue, his wife of 30 years, live in Annapolis, Maryland.

You may write the author at **Write2Us@BooterNation.com**.

Appendix A
Lexicon of Major Concepts & Phrases

"It is the beginning of wisdom to call things by their right names."
- Chinese proverb

Activities of daily living – called ADLs for short, refers to all things we normally do in daily living, including any daily activity that burns calories or requires energy. There are basic **self-care** ADLs, such as bathing, dressing, grooming, and taking medications. There are **instrumental** ADLs, such as doing light housework, preparing meals, shopping, and managing money. ADLs also include any daily activity we perform for **work,** from walking around the office to taking the stairs instead of the elevator, and for **leisure,** from couch potato to hiking and playing tennis.

A fit person will try to maximize his or her ADLs every day. ADL is a term used by a variety of disciplines, from fitness training to nursing, especially in the care of the elderly.

ADLs – See **activities of daily living**

Ageism – refers to prejudice or negative attitudes toward aging in general and to those who are older.

All-ages communities – refers to retirement communities that are progressive, diverse, and located in more urbanized areas preferred by younger homebuyers, who are encouraged to give the community more age diversity.

Amenity migrants - refers to people who migrate to another state or region seeking better weather or an environment with more choices, e.g., in entertainment, the arts, sport, or other recreational activities or work opportunities. See also **lone eagles**.

Belief system – See **worldview**.

Bonus years – refers to the extra post-career years we will enjoy owing to increasing longevity, which increased by two-thirds in the last century.

Boomerang kids – refers to a young person past high-school age who returns home to live after college or a period of independence. As a result of tight job markets, heavy student loan burdens, and other factors, the number of boomerang kids has been increasing. As a result, many "empty nests" are transformed into what some have called a "crowded" or "cluttered" nest.[271]

Boomers – refers to a huge cohort of 78 million Americans born between 1946 and 1964, often visualized as the baby boom pig in the demographic snake. This moving age wave[272] is visible among those with media profiles, but it's even more visible on Main Street throughout America. Now that the boomers are moving into their later-life years, with the first turning 65 in 2011, they will no doubt continue to set the political, economic, and social tone of American society – as they have from the beginning. From hoola hoops, coonskin caps, and fast food, to Woodstock, civil rights, and the peace movement, boomers have influenced America's culture. Boomers have also given us Macintosh, e-Bay, YouTube and diversity in business and politics.[273] Those on the leading edge of the age wave are in for another unique experience as they move into the post-career segment of later life, and the way they react will once again shape our culture. Boomers are moving into their later life in a very changed environment, especially because programs made for later-life Americans, such as Medicare and Social Security, are broke, which may require more Boomers to work longer. To paraphrase Bill Clinton, "Many will go out working."[274]

Booterpreneurs – refers to business owners, such as TCBY founder and CEO, Frank Hickingbotham, who leverage their later-life assets and experiences to start and manage a new venture, reflecting recent findings by the Kauffman Foundation, a nonprofit organization dedicated to the research and support of entrepreneurship, that the highest rate of entrepreneurial activity is found among those between 55 and 64 years old. See also **booters**, **work**.

Booters – refers to post-career individuals who have rebooted, i.e., people who reject the "Golden Years" mythology and, instead, have chosen to incorporate some form of work into their post-career years. See also **Golden Years, post-career, reboot, work**.

Bridge employment – refers to the transition period between full-time work and post-career years. The term was coined by the Health and Retirement Study of the National Institute on Aging to describe a time during which many people work part time, are self-employed, or temporarily employed. See also **tailored work.**

Calling – refers to the purpose for living or the pursuit of a purpose in life. A calling is bigger than a job and involves activities that one finds both fruitful (or productive) and satisfying. We do many things that are satisfying, but not always productive, e.g., golf, sailing, horse shoes. We do many things that are productive but not usually satisfying, e.g., cleaning toilets, shoveling snow, removing rubbish. To a secular person or a New Age spiritual person, pursuit of one's calling is about self-fulfillment or what the psychologist Abraham Maslow called "self-actualization." For those with a Judeo-Christian worldview, a calling does more than give purpose and meaning to life. A calling is how one acts to glorify God, to complete His plan for us.

Career-shifting – refers to taking post-career work in a line of work very different from what had been one's life vocation. Example: The lawyer who becomes a school teacher; the school teacher who becomes a volunteer at the pregnancy clinic.

Cottage industry – refers to an industry where the creation of products and services is home-based, rather than factory-based. Products and services created by cottage industry are often unique and distinctive, reflecting the fact that they are usually not mass-produced.

Desert rat – refers to later-life people who, instead of relocating, spend the winter in Arizona or another southwest Sunbelt state and head back north in the summer, e.g., to northern California or to one of the Rocky Mountain states. For example, go to Lake Dillon or Vail, Colorado, in the summertime and you see license plates from all over the Southwest, but especially from Arizona. Like snowbirds in the East, many desert rats take up permanent residence in Arizona to take advantage of a more hospitable climate, more favorable tax laws, and lower cost of living, even though they will still consider home to be in Colorado, Utah, or California, though more than a few desert rats come from the Midwest and the East. See also **snowbirds**.

Down-shifting – refers to the increasingly widespread practice of post-career work on a reduced schedule, for example, working a half day instead of a full day, two or three days a week, or six to eight months a year. See also **retirement, career-shifting.**

Empty nesters – refers to middle-aged persons whose children have left home, to go to college, get married, or otherwise take up their own life, providing parents with a new life that has more freedom, more choices, fewer demands, and fewer responsibilities.

Geriatrics – refers to a specialty in medicine focusing on the physical disabilities and diseases associated with aging and older persons. Increasingly aging is recognized as a normal process, not a disease state.

Gerontology – refers to the study of aging from a broad perspective, including but not limited to the clinical and biological aspects of aging, and the social, psychosocial, economic, historic, and political realms.

Gifts – refers to the generic gifts of time, talent, and treasure. Time is the most precious of the three because time is the only gift, which, once spent, is gone forever. Talent can be in our genes but it can also be learned and nurtured. Talent includes things such as artistic ability, manual skills, and life skills – from compassion to carpentry – that people are born with or develop over the course of their life. Treasure includes money but also other assets, such as gifts of the intellect, e.g., wisdom, understanding, knowledge, and counsel; gifts of the spirit, such as courage, fortitude, and piety.

Great Recession – refers to the global financial crisis that included a steep decline in housing prices and a stock market crash from a Dow of 14,000-plus to a Dow of 6,600 in 2009. As a result, the net worth of millions of Americans was sharply diminished, creating a special challenge for later-life Americans who don't have time to make it up, or wait until the market comes back. Though by the winter of 2010, equities had regained about 70 to 80 percent of their pre-crash values, home equity losses, exceeding more than

$1.0 trillion, did not recover, as housing prices remained depressed and home foreclosures continued.

Homing pigeons – refers to post-career Americans who pick up and move after they retire and then return home after they find that paradise wasn't all it was cracked up to be.[275] See also **lone eagles, rovers.**

Knowledge worker – refers to anyone who works for a living at tasks that involve developing or using specialized knowledge and information. The term is used to include people whose jobs include researching, writing, analyzing, or advising, such as teachers, librarians, analysts, brokers, technical writers, journalists, doctors, nurses, lawyers, accountants, marketing specialists, architects, scientists of all kinds, students of all kinds, and others who specialize in information processing to make a living. It also includes those in the information technology (IT) fields, such as programmers, systems analysts, and others involved in planning, acquiring, searching, analyzing, organizing, storing, programming, distributing, or otherwise contributing to the transformation and commerce of information. The term was first used by Peter Drucker in his 1959 book, *Landmarks of Tomorrow.*[276]

Later life – refers to people in the 50-plus age group, what sociologists call an age cohort. The words and phrases we presently use to describe people in later life are terrible. Think of them: Seniors, elders, oldsters, geezers, gummers, retirees, over-the-hill, advanced age. And the phrases we use to describe these years are equally awful, such as twilight years, golden years, sunset years, Sabbath years, sabbatical years. Later life can and should be a great time of life, a time when one draws on and passes on the knowledge, experience, and wisdom gained over many years, in each day, week, month, or year of what should and can be the most creative and rewarding period of life.

Leisure – refers to time during which a person has no work responsibilities, that is, no obligations or accountabilities, and therefore is free to engage in totally optional activity. Social scientists view leisure as "free time" for people to spend in activities unrelated to employment, housework, or self-care. Defined this way, leisure time may be interesting or dull, depending on the activities carried out in that time. When the activity is pleasurable, free or leisure time is called recreation. However, as Augustine said, "The attraction of a life of leisure ought not to be the prospect of lazy inactivity, but the chance for the investigation and discovery of truth, on the understanding that each person makes some progress in this, and does not grudgingly withhold his discoveries from another."[277] See **also pastime, recreation.**[278]

Lingering death – refers to the kind of death that large numbers of Americans face, characterized by a prolonged period of progressive illness and disability before death. Prior to World War II and even into the post-War era, people typically died on the job or after a short illness, when serious illness more often arrived with little warning and, within days or weeks, people either lived through it or died. In fact, serious illnesses and disabilities were common at every age, and dying was quick. No longer. Today, growing numbers face lingering death, which imposes huge financial and psychological costs on the family and growing financial pressures on the public treasury. [279]

Lone eagles – refers to people who live by their wits and seek a new life by moving to a new location after they retire. Lone eagles tend to move to one of America's celebrated retirement meccas, for example, the American Southwest, the west coast of Florida, the Ozarks, or the barrier islands off the coast of the Carolinas. However, fewer than 10 percent of post-career Americans move. Most stay put where they have family, friends, and networks of support for the activities of daily living.[280]

Mindset – See **worldview.**

N4A – refers to the National Association of Area Agencies on Aging, called N4A, a Washington, D.C.-based advocacy group. N4A is an umbrella organization to ensure that needed resources and support services are available to older Americans.

Off the clock – refers to post-career years when one no longer desires or has the ability to work, when one gives up obligations and accountabilities to others. Also referred to as Script 2.0. See also **on the clock, Script 2.0.**

Old-Age, Survivors and Disability Insurance (OASDI) – refers to a federal program under the Social Security Act, providing benefits to eligible individuals who are fully insured, have reached entitlement age, and have applied for retirement insurance benefits, or to those persons who are the eligible survivors of the deceased, insured worker.

Older Americans Act (OAA) – refers to legislation designed to ensure full participation for later-life Americans in all aspects of society. Defines 10 objectives, or rights for later-life persons, creates the Administration on Aging (AoA), authorizes a variety of social and nutrition programs, provides for the development and implementation of training, research and multidisciplinary gerontology centers, promotes community service employment opportunities for later-life Americans, and authorizes grants to tribal organizations for social and nutritional services. The OAA is amended every three years.

On the clock – refers to that time of life when one's career is over, but one still is engaged in work of some kind, in activities that involve obligations to perform and accountabilities to others. Being on the clock is not about age, physical dexterity or mental acuity. It is about a person's gifts and their desire and ability to take on obligations to use them to help others or make the world a better place. Also referred to as Script 1.0. See also **off the clock, Script 1.0**.

Pastime – refers to an activity that occupies one's spare time pleasantly or with pleasure, from daydreaming and reading to sailing or playing golf. See **also recreation.**

Post-career later life – refers to the later-life years after one retires from career work. For those who take early retirement, the post-career years may begin at age 45, 50, or 55. For most, the post-career years begin on average at age 62. For many others, however, the post-career years will be delayed till age 65, 67, or even later.

Reboot – refers to restarting or remaking something. In computing, when a computer quits working the way it should, the operator turns it off, pauses, and turns it back on. That allows the computer to reboot the operating system that makes it run. Or sometimes one buys new software applications, such as desktop publishing, expense tracking, or games, in order to make the computer serve *the owner's* needs and purposes. One loads new software and then reboots. In television serials, reboot means to discard some or all of a TV series and start anew with fresh plots, personalities, or sets. Examples include *Sesame Street, CSI, Grey's Anatomy, Jeopardy, Wheel of Fortune.* Through reboots, film franchises are revamped and reinvigorated to attract new fans and stimulate economic revenue, providing a way to rescue franchises that have grown stale. Examples include *Tarzan, Rocky, Godfather, Batman,*

Star Trek, Superman, and James Bond-inspired movies, comic books, and video games.

Recreation – refers to free-time activity that is pleasurable. Recreation may include daydreaming, walking in city parks, socializing with neighbors, reading, listening to the radio, watching TV, arts and crafts or other hobbies, trekking, skiing, scuba diving, etc. The ability to engage in recreational activities depends, first and foremost, on having the time (time off, spare time, free time, a holiday, R&R) and then, depending on the activity, the money.[281] See **also pastime, leisure.**

Religion – refers to a system of beliefs about order in the universe and our relationship to it, typically including reverence for a supernatural power (e.g., God or an Essence or Source) that is regarded as creator and/or sovereign of the universe. Religions typically have a **belief system** (often referred to as a creed and sometimes written down in a catechism that is used for instruction), a system of **celebrations** (e.g., for a Christian, the sacraments, such as confirmation, marriage, communion), a **code to live by** (e.g., for Jews and Christians, the Ten Commandments), and sometimes mantras or **special prayers** (e.g., for Jews and Christians, the Lord's Prayer).[282] Some religions, for example, Shintoism and the pagan religions of the ancient Greco-Roman period have celebrations and codes to live by but rely on secular philosophy or other sources to explain the meaning and purpose of life.[283] According to William James, in his *Varieties of Religious Experience*, "...religion says that there is an unseen order, and our supreme good lies in rightful relations to it."[284]

Retirement – refers to the withdrawal of individuals from the labor force, often at a certain age, typically between ages 55 and 65.[285] Withdrawal may be involuntary, owing to health conditions or a compulsory retirement age, or it may be voluntary, for example, to pursue other work or leisure or to escape a distasteful job or the high pressure and stress of many modern-day jobs. See also **career-shifting, revolving retirement.**

Retirement Living TV – See **RLTV.**

Revolving retirement – refers to people who cycle in and out of work in their post-career years.

RLTV – refers to *Retirement Living TV,* the Emmy award-winning cable network dedicated to serving adults 50-plus by providing information and entertainment reflecting the needs and lifestyles of later-life Americans. RLTV programming covers healthcare, finance, travel, lifestyle, comedy, and drama.

Rovers – refers to people who take extended travel, often in an RV or motor home, or sometimes even move to a new location after retirement. See **also lone eagles, homing pigeons.**

Sandwich generation – refers to boomers whose lifestyle is influenced by a side-effect of longevity that requires many simultaneously to care for the needs of elderly parents while still supporting their own children, including boomerang kids.

SCORE – refers to the Service Corps of Retired Executives, an important source of free and confidential business and management advice for entrepreneurs and small business owners. SCORE, founded in 1964 as a resource partner with the U.S. Small Business Administration (SBA), is a nonprofit association with 364 chapters and 12,400 volunteers throughout the United States. SCORE volunteers include both working and retired executives, along with business owners who serve as business counselors donating time, wisdom, lessons learned, and other expertise.

Semi-retirement – refers to an increasingly widespread practice of post-career working on a reduced schedule, for example, working six to eight months a year, or three or four days a week, or half a day instead of a full day. See also **retirement, downshifting, career-shifting.**

Spiritual freedom – refers to the virtue of self-awareness, identified by psychologist David Guttmann, who observed that later life is a time when we begin to "run out of excuses" leading to a greater willingness to be honest with ourselves, less prone to escape to illusions, and more accepting "without mercy" of our faults and shortcomings.

Spirituality – refers to vision, love, and the search for answers to the big questions, such as the meaning and purpose of life and relationships with and commitments to God (or an equivalent transcendent being), community, the environment, oneself, the quality of life, life balances and the integration of life, wholeness, and other hungers of the heart. Many people address their spirituality in the context of religion. Others, such as New Agers, reject religion and search for the answers to big questions through reason-based spirituality.[286]

Script 1.0 – refers to the first phase of one's post-career life, beginning when one's career ends and post-career years begin. One continues in Script 1.0 for as long as he or she has the ability, desire, and opportunity to work in some capacity, then moves to Script 2.0 and an off-the-clock status. See also **on the clock, off the clock, Script 2.0.**

Script 2.0 – refers to the second phase of one's post-career life when one loses the desire or ability to work. Script 2.0 is most often associated with frailty or disability. See also **off the clock, on the clock, Script 1.0.**

Scripted life – refers to the idea that our day-to-day life is programmed (or scripted) not from cradle to grave, but instead only from cradle until we leave our place in the workforce. As an infant and youngster, we are scripted by our parents; when we go to school we are scripted by teachers and peers. When we enter the workplace and later, for most, marriage, we are scripted by bosses and the institutional requirements of work and family. Then as we retire, we are suddenly free from the scripts of life. Though from a distance we see this period as freedom, when we are in it, it can be disorienting, rootless, and alienating. See also **unscripted life.**

Snowbirds – refers to later-life people who go south in the winter and return north in the summer, as an alternative to relocation. For example, Sanibel Island or Forth Myers Beach on Florida's west coast sports license plates from all the Great Lakes states, Minnesota to Pennsylvania and New York, and from Ontario and other parts of Canada as well. Many snowbirds take up permanent residence in Florida to take advantage of a more hospitable climate, favorable tax laws, and lower cost of living, even though they will still consider home to be in Indiana, Ohio or Wisconsin. See also **desert rats**.

Successful aging – refers to how well one lives in later life, not to longevity. Successful aging is about living a good life – one that provides a sense of fulfillment, of being valued, of being cared for, and the sense that one is liked and doing something good for others. Living well for as long as possible and then passing on quickly, avoiding a lingering death, is an important element of successful aging. In a study that has influenced research on aging for more than a decade, the MacArthur Foundation defined successful aging as "... the ability to maintain three key behaviors or characteristics: (1) low risk of disease and disease-related disability; (2) high mental and physical function; (3) active engagement with life...Successful aging...involves activity, which we have labeled engagement with life. Active engagement with life takes many forms, but successful aging is most concerned with two – relationships with other people, and behavior that is productive...It is this forward-looking, active engagement with life and with other human beings that is so critical to growing old well."[288]

Syndrome X – refers to a cluster of chronic illnesses that includes diabetes, renal disease, stroke, hypertension, cancer, and heart disease. As people grow older, some die with four or five of these chronic illnesses.[287]

Tailored work – refers to work customized to reflect our deepest desires and the highest and best use of our gifts of time, talent, and treasure. See also **gifts**.

Time – see **gifts.**

Time-out – refers to the point in the transition process when we let go of or redefine the old and invent a new image of the future. The idea of letting go of the old originated with change management guru Bill Bridges, who calls it the neutral zone. Others who write about change management, transitions, and transformations also use the concepts of unlearning and, learning (Richard Bolles), moratorium and weaning (David Corbett), limbo, and others. See **also transition.**

Transition – refers to what change management guru Bill Bridges calls the "psychological process people go through to come to terms with a new situation." Bridges distinguishes between change and transition. "Change is situational: the new site, the new boss, the new team roles, the new policy. Transition is...external... [and] depends on letting go of the old reality and old identity you had before the change took place." The same goes for organizations: "Nothing so undermines organizational change as the failure to think through who will have to let go of what when change occurs."[289] Bridges calls this time-out between A (what we were before we retired) and B (what we want to become post-career) a neutral zone, which is one of three stages of any transition: (1) The Ending, (2) The Neutral Zone, and, in time, (3) The New Beginning. We know from research on transitions that most people don't just move from Condition A (e.g., working) to Condition B (e.g., a post-career life) without going through a psychological transition. We really go from A to a neutral zone (called here a *time-out*) where we can think things over and adjust to new realities before we move to B. See **also time-out.**

Treasure – see **gifts.**

Unscripted life – refers to that segment of life that arrives the first day of retirement. All of a sudden, after living a life scripted by parents, peers, spouses, bosses, and schedules, – one wakes up to a life with no requirements and few scheduled activities (except health care appointments). The major challenge of later life is to develop a script that will permit one to be productive and satisfied with life – satisfaction that most often comes with using one's gifts to create, assist others, or help make things work. See also **successful aging.**

White House Conference on Aging (WHCOA) – refers to a national conference called to review existing policies that affect later-life Americans and to make recommendations on how those policies can be strengthened and improved. The first national Conference on Aging was held in 1950. Subsequent White House Conferences on Aging have been held in 1961, 1971, 1981, and 1995.

Work – refers to purposeful activities, both mental and physical, that are productive and satisfying and where there are obligations and accountabilities to perform. Work is an activity to which people devote their gifts of time, talent, and energy on a regular basis, a pursuit that yields a beneficial result for themselves, those around them, or the larger society. Work also has spiritual and religious overtones. Both secular and spiritual people see work as purposeful. However, the Judeo-Christian idea of work goes a step further, targeting a specific purpose of work, which is to glorify God. *Reboot!* identifies five types of work: work for pay, creating products or providing services for compensation; in-kind work, trading time and services for in-kind benefits; volunteer work, providing a gifted service or benefit without compensation; Samaritan work, providing generous person-to-person care to another; and enrichment work, taking a disciplined and purposeful approach to self-improvement. Work can be full time or part time. Also, because of the digital revolution, work in today's America can be performed in many locations: at home or the office, in the field or factory, or with the rapid growth of the mobile Internet, on the run.

World of work – refers to the obligations and accountabilities that are core elements of a work situation and the cultures surrounding the venues where work is performed. Just as work is bigger than a job, the world of work is bigger than the office or the factory. The world of work today includes many venues: the home, including the so-called small-office/home-office advanced by the SOHO movement; the hotel business center and other so-called "third places;" the traditional factory, office, or farm as well as difference types of work, such as a part-time paid job; volunteering; etc. So when we say we are going to quit work or retire from work, we are revealing a very narrow (and unrealistic) view of the world of work, the workplace, and work itself. The world of work is anyplace where, in the context of obligations and accountabilities, we apply our gifts to help others or seek to make the world a better place.

Worldview – refers to our overall perspective or collection of beliefs about life and the universe, our assumptions about how the world works, or what others refer to as mindset, philosophy, belief system, religion, or *Weltanschauung*. A worldview is a framework of ideas and attitudes about the world, our place in it, the status of human beings, and life in general, – a comprehensive system of beliefs that provide answers for a wide range of questions: What are humans, why we are here, and what is our purpose in life, how are we advantaged/disadvantaged, what is the course of history... and what can we know and how do we know it? There are religious worldviews (e.g., Christian, Islamic, Hindu) and secular worldviews (e.g., scientific, legal, historic, humanist).

BIBLIOGRAPHIC NOTE

A flood of books, magazines, workshops, and TV programs on some aspect of retirement has been stimulated by the realization that the first of 78 million boomers are turning 65 in 2011. However nearly all the books are either collections of stories about successful retirees or books dealing with some combination of wealth, health, or lifestyle – or public policy/societal trends.

For analytical studies of aging from a societal point of view, the classic book on aging trends and conditions in America is: Ken Dychtwald and Joe Fowler, *The Age Wave:How the Most Important Trend of Our Time Can Change Your Future*, New York: St. Martin's Press, 1988. See also Alan Pifer and Lydia Bronte (eds.), *Our Aging Society: Paradox and Promise*, New York: W.W. Norton, 1986, for an early anthology that is intriguing to read today because the contributors got a lot of it right.

Story-telling is also a favored way to address issues of later life and retirement. Case studies or vignettes abound of how people and families cope with the challenges of aging and life in their post-career years. One of the earliest positive books with interesting stories about aging individuals is Helen Hayes, *Our Best Years*, Garden City, NY: Doubleday, 1984. See also William A. Sadler, *The Third Age: Six Principles for Growth and Renewal after Forty,* Cambridge, Mass.: Perseus Books, 2000.

Several excellent books present the subject of successful aging to general audiences. These include:

- Buzan, Tony and Raymond Keene, *The Age Heresy: You Can Achieve More – Not Less – As You Get Older*, London: Ebury Press, 1996. (One of the earliest research-based books written for a non-academic audience to take a positive view of aging.)[290]
- Hudson, Frederic M., *The Adult Years: Mastering the Art of Self-Renewal*, San Francisco: Jossey-Bass, 1991.

- Rowe, John W., and Robert L Kahn, *Successful Aging,* New York: Pantheon Books, 1998. (Often referred to as *the MacArthur Foundation Study*.)
- Vaillant, George, *Aging Well: Surprising Guideposts to a Happier Life*, New York: Little, Brown, 2002. (Often referred to as *the Harvard Medical School Study*.)
- A holistic approach to later life and planning your post-career years can be found in the following, any one of which is worth reading:
- Bronfman, Edgar M. *The Third Act: Reinventing Yourself after Retirement.* New York: Putnam's, 2002.
- Buettner, Dan. *The Blue Zones: Lessons for Living Longer from the People Who've Lived the Longest.* Washington, DC: National Geographic, 2008.
- Buford, Bob. *Half Time: Moving from Success to Significance.* Grand Rapids: Zondervan, 2009; and his *Finishing Well: What People Who Really Live Do Differently.* Brentwood, TN: Integrity Publishers, 2004; and his *Game Plan: Winning Strategies for the Second Half of Your Life.* Grand Rapids: Zondervan, 1997.
- Corbett, David, with Richard Higgins. *Portfolio Life: The New Path to Work, Purpose, and Passion after 50.* San Francisco: Jossey-Bass, 2007.
- Dychtwald, Ken and Daniel J. Kadlec. *A New Purpose: Redefining Money, Family, Work, Retirement, and Success*, New York: HarperCollins, 2009.
- Freedman, Marc. *Encore: Finding Work That Matters in the Second Half of Life.* New York: Public Affairs, 2008; and his earlier *Prime Time: How Baby Boomers Will Revolutionize Retirement and Transform America.* New York: Public Affairs, 2002.
- Pollan, Stephen M. and Mark Levine. *Second Acts: Creating the Life You Really Want, Building the Career You Truly Desire.* New York: HarperCollins, 2003.
- Sadler, William A. and James H. Kreft, *Changing Course: Navigating Life after 50*, Centennial, Colo.: Center for Third Age Leadership Press, 2007.
- Sedlar, Jeri and Rick Miners, *Don't Retire, Rewire!,* Indianapolis: Alpha/Penguin, 2003.
- Trafford, Abigail. *My Time: Making the Most of the Rest of Your Life.* New York: Basic Books, 2004.

The best among these from the point of view presented in *Reboot!* are Corbett and Higgins' *Portfolio Life* and Marc Freedman's *Encore* and his earlier *Prime Time.* Each of these authors envisions a new kind of aging where post-career Americans remain actively engaged in purposeful activities outside the home, including work, even among those whose financial situation is stable and secure.

A growing number of books on longevity is also useful. A recent and popular example is Dan Buettner, *The Blue Zone*, Washington, D.C.: National Geographic, 2008. Buettner identified those places in the world where people have unusually long lives, such as Sardinia, Italy; Okinawa, Japan; Loma Linda, California; and the Nicoya Peninsula, Costa Rica; and concluded *it is lifestyle, not DNA, that leads to long life.* See also Richard J. Flanigan and Kate Flanigan Sawyer, *Longevity Made Simple: How to Add 20 Good Years to Your Life,* Milwaukee: Williams Clark Publishing, 2007, based on "lessons from decades of research" from which are derived 10 guidelines: (1) lower cholesterol, (2) lower blood pressure, (3) avoid tobacco, (4) eat a diet rich in fish, fruit and vegetables, (5) get exercise, (6) maintain a healthy weight, (7) prevent accidents, (8) drink alcohol, daily in small amounts, (9) take aspirin, and (10) take a multivitamin. However, learning how to extend your life begs the question "for what purpose?" That, of course, is the central question that needs to be answered to achieve successful aging.

Self-help materials abound to help later-life Americans through their time-out. For guidance on how to discover your calling, it is hard to beat the very useful discussion and exercises in Richard N. Bolles, *What Color is Your Parachute? 2010: A Practical Manual for Job-Hunters and Career-Changers*, Berkeley: Ten Speed Press, 2010, especially Chapter 11, pp. 155-241. Also see Kevin and Kay Marie Brennfleck, *Live Your Calling: A Practical Guide to Finding and Fulfilling Your Mission in Life,* San Francisco: Jossey-Bass, 2005, for a terrific set of do-it-yourself exercises that you can use to create your Life Calling Map. The map has four parts: (1) mission statements, (2) dimensions of my design, (3) priority goals, and (4) action plan, and includes assessments of transferable skills, personality, spiritual gifts, and the like.

For simple exercises designed to help you decide what kind of work you might do in your post-career life, see Donald G. Zytowski, "Do You Know What You Would Like?" in Caroline Bird, *Second Careers: New Ways to Work After 50*, Boston: Little Brown, 1992. Bird points out that later-life workers often have work opportunities even in a down economy because workers over 50 have (1) lower absenteeism, (2) higher work ethic, (3) higher productivity, (4) less alcoholism and drug use, (5) steadier, more patient approach to work and interpersonal relations, (6) more job stability, less job hopping, and (7) a willingness to learn.

The growing number of online resources is especially important to the do-it-yourself time-out. In addition to Bolles' *What Color is Your Parachute?* one of the most useful can be found in Ken Dychtwald and Daniel J. Kadlec, *A New Purpose: Redefining Money, Family, Work, Retirement, and Success*, New York: HarperCollins, 2009, beginning on p. 247. Nearly 200 web sites are clustered under useful headings, including sites for (1) crafting your own experience, (2) finding meaningful work, (3) basic service options, (4) activists, (5) mentors, (6) philanthropy, (7) continued personal growth, etc.

For an introduction to the larger idea of calling, see Os Guinness, *Rising to the Call: Discover the Ultimate Purpose of Your Life.* Nashville: Thomas Nelson, 2003, or a brief introduction in his "How Do I Build a Successful Life and Career?" in Joe Gibbs, *Game Plan for Life: Your Personal Playbook for Success.* Carol Stream, Ill: Tyndale, 2009. See also his *Entrepreneurs of Life: Faith and the Venture of Purposeful Living,* Colorado Springs: NavPress, 2001. For a practical application of callings, see Kevin and Kay Marie Brennfleck, *Live Your Calling: A Practical Guide to Finding and Fulfilling Your Mission in Life,* noted above.

ENDNOTES

Preface

1 David Walker, Comeback America: Turning the Country Around and Restoring Fiscal Responsibility, New York: Random House, 2009, p. 70. From 1998-2008, Walker served as the US Comptroller General and CEO of the Government Accountability Office and is now the president of the Peterson Foundation.

2 AARP is formerly known as the American Association of Retired Persons.

3 Harry R. Moody, "The Search for Meaning in Later Life," The Gerontologist, (vol. 49) 2009, pp. 856-859.

4 I did, however, once flirt with policy issues of aging. I was exposed early in my career to the issues surrounding aging and gerontology when I was director of the Behavioral Sciences Laboratory at The Ohio State University. Owing to the kind of research performed in the lab I directed, I was selected to serve on the national planning group for the 1970 White House Conference on Aging, chaired by Arthur Fleming, and convened by President Nixon and the Administration on Aging. Planning for and participating in the White House Conference on Aging was a rich experience. As I have returned to this subject nearly 40 years later, it is encouraging to see how much progress has been made, and it is interesting to recognize some names of real experts I knew for a fleeting moment in a previous life.

1. Charter a Course in Later Life

5 Internal Revenue Service, Individual Retirement Arrangements for use in preparing 2009 returns, (Pub.590), January 2, 2010, pp. 90-91. For an estimate of life expectancy customized to your lifestyle, see http://www.worldlifeexpectancy.com/le_test.php

6 For reasons discussed in Chapter 2, later life is the term we use for what others call elders, oldsters, retirees, geezers, gummers and other commonly used terms for Americans over 50.

7 I was born in mid-1939, seven years ahead of the first boomers, born in 1946.

8 Actually, 10,000 a day is an average. It is a lower number in the beginning and peaks in 2025. This year, according to the US Census Bureau, only about 7,600 people will turn 65 each day; in 2025, the total projected is about 11,700 a day.

9 A useful and now widely used term coined by aging guru Ken Dychtwald, a pioneer in getting us to think about the impact of aging boomers on American culture. See Ken Dychtwald and Joe Fowler, The Age Wave: How The Most Important Trend of Our Time Can Change Your Future, New York: St. Martin's Press, 1988.

10 See, for example, books with titles like Half Time, Prime Time, My Time, Second Act, The Third Act, Changing Lanes, Changing Course, and Finishing Well, which are among the

more useful in addressing some of the central issues of successful aging, not the least, the importance of continued social engagement to achieve a successful transition to post-career years. For a listing of the most helpful, see Appendix B.

11   John W. Rowe and Robert L Kahn, Successful Aging, New York: Pantheon Books, 1998, p. 49, and also Chapter 10, pp. 152-66. These issues are addressed by George Vaillant, Aging Well: Surprising Guideposts to a Happier Life, New York: Little, Brown, 2002, for example, pp. 203-211, 278-79, 308; and Tony Buzan and Raymond Keene, The Age Heresy: You Can Achieve More – Not Less – As You Get Older, London: Ebury Press, 1996, for example, p. 121. For an empathic account of how we change, grow, and learn in later life, see insightful story-telling about later-life Americans in Sara Lawrence-Lightfoot, The Third Chapter: Passion, Risk, and Adventures in the 25 Years after 50, New York: Sara Crichton Books, 2009.

12   John W. Rowe and Robert L. Kahn, Successful Aging, op. cit., p. 51.

13   George Vaillant, Aging Well, op. cit.

14   Dan Buettner, The Blue Zone, Washington, D.C.: National Geographic, 2008. Buettner identified those places in the world where people have unusually long lives, such as Sardinia, Italy; Okinawa, Japan; Loma Linda, California; the Nicoya Peninsula, Costa Rica; and Ikaria, Greece, and concluded it is lifestyle, not DNA, that leads to long life. The Blue Zone summarizes nine lessons learned from the lifestyles of people in these four areas that allow them to live longer and healthier lives, such as putting their families first, belonging to a faith-based community, and having a sense of purpose.

15   Discussed further in Chapter 15. For a discussion of the advantages of later life and the assets we bring to it, see Gene D. Cohen, The Creative Age: Awakening Human Potential in the Second Half of Life, New York: HarperCollins/Avon Books, 2001.

16   On these points about language and thinking and the importance of framing and fencing issues, see George Lakoff, Moral Politics : How Liberals and Conservatives Think, Chicago: University of Chicago Press, 2002, and Frank Luntz, Words That Work: It's Not What You Say, It's What People Hear, New York: Hyperion, 2008.

17   Some of the newer substitutes are not much better – rebounders, graduates, or re-careerers. On the other hand, I think we are stuck with senior because it is so widely used, and it's not that bad. I'm also comfortable with old-soldier, war-horse, old hand, and old salt, because they imply positive attributes – and they sure beat words like mossback, old dog, and gummer.

18   Internal Revenue Service, Individual Retirement Arrangements for use in preparing 2009 returns, (Pub.590), January 2, 2010, pp. 90-91.

19   We are rapidly entering a new, older world among the developed nations, where, at the beginning of the 20th century, one in 700 was over age 80; by the middle of this century it will be closer to one in seven. Tony Buzan and Raymond Keene, The Age Heresy, op. cit., p. 169.

20 See, for example, John W. Rowe and Robert L Kahn, Successful Aging, op. cit., Chapter 1, especially pp. 26-28; George Vaillant, Aging Well, op. cit.; and Tony Buzan and Raymond Keene, The Age Heresy, op. cit. For an empathic account of how we change, grow, and learn in later life, see insightful story-telling about later-life Americans in Sara Lawrence-Lightfoot, The Third Chapter, op. cit.

21 See, for example, the mind sports and other exercises in Tony Buzan and Raymond Keene, The Age Heresy, op. cit. Psychologist Erik Erikson is generally regarded as the first social scientist to view adult development as progress, not decline. See his Childhood and Society, New York: W.W. Norton, 1950.

22 For different views on this issue, see Richard D. Thau and Jay S. Heflin (eds.), Generations Apart: Xers vs. Boomers vs. the Elderly. Amherst, NY: Prometheus Books, 1997.

23 There are many recent examples of later-life workers, such as management guru Peter Drucker (who was active as a teacher, writer, and advisor into his nineties), Pulitzer Prize winning author James Michener (who wrote the first of more than two dozen books at age 41), and Winston Churchill who was named Prime Minister the second time at 77 and was active into his nineties. President Bush (#41) celebrated his 80th birthday (and birthdays since) by parachuting from an airplane; John Glenn, former US Senator and first American to orbit the earth in 1963, orbited the earth again in 1999, at the age of 77, 36 years after his first flight. For an interesting review of what people accomplish in later life, see Mark Washburn, When I was Your Age: An Irreverent Guide to Who Did What and When, at Every Age (Well, Only 4-90), Naperville, Ill: Sourcebooks, Inc., 2006.

24 For a touching account of the process of aging from the perspective of a participant-observer, a woman who is herself absorbed in the process, see Lillian L. Hawthorne. Finishing Touches: An Insightful Look into the Mirror of Aging. Forest Knolls, Calif.: Elder Books, 1998.

25 Mindfulness is always important but especially during times of transition. See Ronald D. Siegel, The Mindfulness Solution: Everyday Practices for Everyday Problems, New York: Guilford Press, 2010, and especially Chapter 10 on aging, pp. 283-314.

26 See Darragh Johnson, "An Old Salt's Sea Change," The Washington Post (Style Section), July 12, 2005, for an account of how we changed our boating preference from sail to power. For this heresy, the reporter called us "transvesselites." It was a short-lived experiment. After passages that included the canals of New York, the Great Lakes, and rivers of the Northeast, we became recidivists, shifting back to sail.

27 See, for example, William Bridges, Managing Transitions: Making the Most of Change, New York: Addison-Wesley, 1991. This was my first exposure to the thinking and writing of Bill Bridges. The Center itself is an impressive institution, annually serving more than 20,000 individuals and 2,000 organizations, including more than 80 of the Fortune 100 companies and other public, private, nonprofit and education sectors.

28   Reference here is to Telstra Corporation, Ltd., Australia's leading provider of telecom-
     munications services and one of the nation's top business enterprises with, at the time,
     55,000 employees and $25 billion in annual revenues.

29   At the time, my wife was working as a college and career counselor at the Annapolis
     Area Christian School (AACS) and could not responsibly leave on short notice. Still, she
     was as eager as I was to get me suited up and back on the field – and, truth be told, out
     of the house. So three days later I left for Sydney, and my wife joined me a few months
     later.

30   See Holman Jenkins, "Australia's Broadband Blunder," The Wall Street Journal,
     November 3, 2009, for an insightful assessment of our work in Australia, including our
     effort to stop the folly of an intrusive government trying to nationalize the governance
     of a newly privatized corporation owned by 1.4 million Aussie shareholders.

2. The Onset of Later Life

31   It is noteworthy that the AARP dropped the longer name (as IBM dropped International
     Business Machines decades ago), in part to avoid the inapt word "retired."

32   Modern Maturity was started in 1958 and ran until 2002 when it was replaced by AARP,
     The Magazine, a bi-monthly publication of AARP that focuses on aging issues. The
     magazine is sent to every AARP member, and by some counts is the largest circulation
     magazine in the world. Largest or not, the competently edited magazine deals with
     important issues of later life in a timely and fact-based way.

33   Dora L. Costa, History of Retirement, Chicago: University of Chicago Press,
     1998, pp. 9-14.

34   Dora L. Costa, History of Retirement, Ibid.

35   The FDR-era longevity adjustment is calculated on the ratio of 62:65 = 78:82. If we go
     back to 1888 and perform a "Bismarck longevity adjustment", today's retirement age
     would be 112 years (!), reflecting the ratio of 45:65 is equivalent to 78:112.

36   See, for example, Gillette Edmunds, How to Retire Early and Live Well with Less Than a
     Million Dollars, Avon, Mass.: Adams Media, 2000.

37   In addition to the 2010 Census, see Carole Fleck, "Is Retirement Even Possible?
     Millions of People 70+ Are Still on the Job." AARP. September 1, 2009; Murray Gendell,
     "Retirement Age Declines Again in 1990s." Monthly Labor Review. October 2001;
     "RAND Study Predicts More Americans Will Delay Retirement; Trend Will Help Bolster
     Social Security and Medicare." Ascribe Newswire: Health. April 7, 2010; and S.K. Brown,
     "Attitudes of individuals 50 and older toward phased retirement," (2005) see www.
     aarp.org/research/reference/publicopinions/attitudes

38   In fact, a recent study shows that 55 percent of people age 60 to 64 were in the labor
     market during the first 11 months of 2010, up from 47 percent for the same period in
     2000. Dennis Cauchon, "American workforce growing grayer," USA Today, December
     15, 2010.

39 See the Age Discrimination in Employment Act (ADEA) of 1978, which prohibits age discrimination in hiring, discharges, lay-offs, promotions, wages, and other areas of employment. A key ADEA rule, which applies to workplaces with more than 20 employees, is that no worker can be forced to retire. But there are now many exceptions, owing to subsequent amendments, such as ADEA Amendments of 1986, which permits tenured college/university professors to be forced to retire at age 70. Other exceptions where mandatory retirement is permitted include certain police and fire employees, federal law enforcement and air traffic control employees, and anyone in a job, such as piloting an airplane, where age and physical or mental dexterity are a reasonable occupational qualification.

40 It is interesting to note that retirement is mentioned only once in the Judeo-Christian scriptures – Numbers 8:24-26 in the NIV Bible (New International Version). There the recommended retirement age is 50 – though retirees are admonished to continue to assist their brothers in community service. So even in our most ancient documents it is hard to find the idea that the natural cycle of life is to be born, work, retire and die.

3. The Comfort of a Scripted Life.

41 What I call scripting is what the social scientists call socialization, which refers to "the process by which people learn culture, roles, and norms in order to function within a society. The socialization of culture includes learning the language, beliefs, social structure and institutions of the culture in which an individual lives." See "Socialization" in the International Encyclopedia of the Social Sciences (both for 1968 and 2008).

42 In 1981, Dorothy Miller coined the term "sandwich generation" to refer to the middle-aged generation that provides support to both younger and older family members. Miller emphasized the unique stress of multigenerational care-giving, where the burden often falls disproportionately on women who serve multiple demanding roles of wife, mother, daughter, care-giver, and employee. See http://family.jrank.org/pages/1446/Sandwich-Generation-Definition.html#ixzzOXH1bloPx Today, owing to increasing longevity, some estimate that as many as 50 percent of American families span four generations.

43 See John A. Byrne, "Working for the Boss from Hell," Fast Company, December 2007.

4. Entering the Unscripted Life

44 Adopted from Marie Beynon Ray, The Best Years of Your Life, Boston: Little, Brown, 1952., p. 54.

45 Quoted in the magazine, Kennedy School of Government, Autumn 2002, p. 55.

46 Though there is speculation that one of the impacts of the Great Recession that began in December 2007 may be an upward trend in the average age of retirement, as people delay retirement to augment their income. Chris Isidore, "It's official: Recession since Dec. '07: The National Bureau of Economic Research declares what most Americans already knew: the downturn has been going on for some time," CNNMoney.com, December 1, 2008.

47   The impact of new medical technologies and practices is happening at every stage of
     life. See, for example, Sanjay Gupta, Cheating Death: The Doctors and Medical Miracles
     That Are Saving Lives against All Odds, New York: Wellness Central, 2009.

48   From the song, "Go Where You Wanna Go" by songwriter John Phillips. See http://
     www.lyricsfreak.com/m/mamas+the+papas/go+where+you+wanna+go_20087276.
     html

49   For an account of a retired couple who moved to Naples to play golf and enjoy the sun,
     and then returned to Detroit for what they now regard as a much richer life. see Toby
     Barlow, "Snowbirds Come Home to Roost," The New York Times, February 21, 2010. I
     call these people homing pigeons.

50   I've been observing and writing about lone eagles, homing pigeons, and other birds of
     the digital economy for many years. See, for example, Philip M. Burgess, "Lone Eagles
     Nest in the West," Rocky Mountain News, September 15, 1992. The Lone Eagle phenom-
     enon has been widely covered, including an upbeat cover story on the Rocky Mountain
     region in Time (September 16, 1993) and a cover story in Newsweek (May 24, 1994)
     and major stories in Forbes (December 21, 1992), Business Week (November 15, 1993),
     American Demographics magazine (August 1993), Inc. magazine (January 1994), and
     Parade magazine (May 1994).

51   For the warm, fuzzy perspective, see Edward Fays, A Grandparent's Gift of Love: True
     Stories of Comfort, Hope, and Wisdom, New York: Warner Books, 2002. For different
     views from a social science perspective, see Vern L. Bengston and Joan F. Robertson
     (ed.), Grandparenthood, Beverly Hills: Sage, 1985.

52   See, for example, David Bancroft Avrick, "How Many People Move Each Year?"
     DMNews, July 7, 2005. In fact, Brookings Institution demographer Bill Frey reminds us
     that we "used to think of places that attracted seniors as specialized retirement com-
     munities…Now, in effect, most of America will be a 'retirement community.'" Quoted in
     Rob Gurwitt, "Staying Connected," AARP Bulletin, March 2010, p. 26.

53   See "Better Places To Retire," Consumer Report/MoneyAdviser, April 2007. Though
     most post-career Americans stay put, when they do move, they tend to do it for one of
     three reasons: (1) to get closer to kids and grandkids, (2) to live in a better climate or a
     social environment with more choices, that is, amenity migrants, or (3) to reduce living
     expenses, especially taxes and housing costs. See also John Howells, Where to Retire:
     America's Best and Most Affordable Places, Oakland: Gateway Books, 1995, which as-
     sesses locations by affordability, safety, and a host of amenities.

54   John W. Rowe and Robert L Kahn, Successful Aging, op. cit. and George Vaillant, Aging
     Well, op. cit. See also Tom Rath and Jim Hartor, Wellbeing: The Five Essential Elements,
     New York: Gallup Press, 2010, especially Chapter 4, "Physical Wellbeing," pp. 69-89.

55   Kenneth H. Cooper, Aerobics, New York: Bantam Books, 1968. Dr. Cooper is the founder
     of the respected Cooper Aerobics Center in Dallas, Texas, and the author of more than
     20 books on fitness and nutrition. He is also the founder of a research and education

nonprofit called The Cooper Institute, established in 1970. His most recent books are Start Strong, Finish Strong (2007) and Matters of the Heart: Adventures in Sports Medicine (2007).

56   The lingering death that goes on for months and increasingly even years is a new trend in human affairs that most would hope to avoid.

57   See "Special Investors Issue," Fortune, June 2010.

58   See John W. Rowe and Robert L Kahn, Successful Aging, op. cit. Like George Vaillant's Harvard study, this trail-blazing report by the MacArthur Foundation's Study of Aging in America provides strong evidence for the proposition that successful aging is largely determined by lifestyle choices in diet, exercise, the pursuit of mental challenges, self-confidence, and especially social engagement and involvement with other people, and not genetic inheritance.

59   For an outstanding review of how to stay engaged, see Nicole Bouchard Boles, "How to Be an Everyday Philanthropist: 330 ways to make a difference in your home, community and world – at no cost," New York: Workman Publishing, 2009.

5. Pitfalls of the Unscripted Life

60   Quoted in Patricia Suggs, "Ethical Issues in Spiritual Care," in Tanya Fusco Johnson (ed.), Handbook on Ethical Issues in Aging, Westport: Greenwood Press, 1999, p. 81.

61   The phrase bucket list comes from a wonderful comedy about redemption. See Sidebar in Chapter 14.

62   And for those with a faith life, we are, first and foremost, children of God. See Os Guinness, Rising to the Call: Discover the Ultimate Purpose of Your Life. Nashville: Thomas Nelson, 2003.

63   Henri Nouwen, posthumous Home Tonight: Further Reflections on the Parable of the Prodigal Son, New York: Doubleday, 2009, edited by Sue Mosteller, pp. 37 ff.

64   The email from "Joe" is dated May 2, 2010. "Joe" asked me not to use his family's name.

65   For a provocative and insightful discussion of how the culture of authenticity leads us to "do our thing" or find our own fulfillment, see Charles Taylor, The Ethics of Authenticity, Cambridge: Harvard University Press, 1991, pp. 25-53. See also St. Augustine of Hippo, Confessions, New York: Penguin, 1961 (R.S. Pine-Coffin, trans.) for a dramatic account of how one man who changed the world discovered his calling well into his adult life while walking in the forest.

6. Retirement is a Bad Idea

66   Cited in Mitch Anthony, The New Retirementality: Planning Your Life and Dreams...at Any Age You Want, Chicago: Dearborn Financial Publishing, 2001, p.63.

67   Marie Beynon Ray, The Best Years of Your Life, op. cit., p 33.

68   With a career spanning more than 70 years, Helen Hayes (1900-1993) was long con-
      sidered the "First Lady of American Theater." At age 83, she used the radio to become
      an advocate for issues facing the elderly. Her weekly program, The Best Years, urged
      listeners to welcome advancing age, and she used her air time to address new activi-
      ties, opportunities, and challenges for those over 65. Based on J. Martin Klotsche and
      Adolph A. Suppan, Life Begins at Eighty, Milwaukee: The Kenwood Press, 1991, p. 31 and
      Helen Hayes, Our Best Years, New York: Doubleday, 1986. I found several copies of Our
      Best Years on Amazon and bought one. Didn't somebody say, "There is nothing new
      under the sun."

69   Larry Minnix is president of the American Association of Homes and Services for the
      Aging, a nonprofit trade group. Cited in Deborah Kotz, "Get Ready for the Age Wave,"
      USN&WR, February 10, 2010, p. 19.

70   Marc Gunther, "Marriott gets a wake-up call," Fortune, July 6, 2009, p. 66.

71   J.B. Sykes (ed.), The Concise Oxford Dictionary of Current English (Sixth Edition, 11th
      Impression), Oxford: Clarendon Press, 1980, p. 960.

72   See Bob Clyatt, Work Less, Live More: The Way to Semi-Retirement, Berkeley: Nolo,
      2007. See also Gillette Edmunds, "Retire Early and Live Well, Avon, Mass.: Avon Media,
      2000; Timothy Ferriss, The 4-Hour Workweek: Escape 9-5, Live Anywhere, and Join
      the New Rich, New York: Crown, 2007; and Dee Lee and Jim Flewelling, The Complete
      Idiot's Guide to Retiring Early, Indianapolis: Alpha Books, 2001.

73   See, for example, Huston Smith, The World's Religions, New York: HarperOne, 1991, and
      Stephen Prothero, God Is Not One: The Eight Rival Religions That Run the World and
      Why Their Differences Matter, New York: HarperOne, 2010. See also Philip Novak, The
      World's Wisdom: Sacred Texts of the World's Religions, New York: HarperOne, 1994.

74   The Levites, among the 12 tribes of Israel, were priests or their assistants who per-
      formed support roles and secondary duties of the sanctuary service (1 Kings 8:4, Ezra
      2:70).

75   See Numbers 8:24-26 in the NIV Bible (New International Version). Italics added. The
      term used in Scripture is "Tent of Meeting" which refers to a portable sanctuary or
      tabernacle, used by the Hebrews in the wilderness. I have substituted the word "taber-
      nacle" as a more commonly understood term.

76   John 2:1-11 in the New Testament Gospels presents the story of the wedding at Cana,
      where Jesus miraculously turned water into wine. As the story unfolds, there is the
      clear implication that you save the best for last.

77   There are many approaches to retirement living, including independent living, home
      care, adult care, senior housing, assisted living, nursing home, and a continuing-care
      retirement community (which offers most levels of care in the same community). These
      are usefully summarized by the Mayo Clinic at http://www.mayoclinic.com/health/
      long-term-care/HA00054.

78   Americans of all ages increasingly seek the security of gated residential communi-
     ties. In the 1970s there were approximately 2,000 gated communities nationwide. By
     the year 2000, there were over 50,000 gated properties, with more being built every
     year. That equates to about seven million households or six percent of the national
     total behind walls or fences. Based on Chris E. McGoey, "Gated Communities: Access
     Control Issues," from www.crimedoctor.com/gated.htm. The Great Recession, however,
     appears to have stemmed the growth of retirement communities, because (1) retirees
     have a harder time selling their homes into the housing downturn, (2) when they do
     sell, they get less cash than anticipated, and (3) many have suffered major hits to
     their investment portfolios. See Haya El Nasser, "Walls come down on age for over-55
     communities," USA Today, March 22, 2010, p. 1.

79   See www.thevillages.com. This is typical of ad lines used by age-restricted, lifestyle-
     oriented retirement communities. Though post-career Americans seeking play and
     paradise may be the market segment the advertising department puts on the front
     line, The Villages is also described as a "retirement community where people's dreams
     can come true." Still, I know from personal experience that many who are drawn to
     a Villages-type environment dream not only about recreation and pleasure but also
     about service, enrichment, and other forms of work.

80   Dora L. Costa, History of Retirement, op. cit., p. 23.

81   Also, the seniority system, embedded in the rapidly expanding union movement, fa-
     vored older, more expensive workers. So the defined benefit retirement plan was a
     strong countervailing force, providing a compelling incentive for more senior workers
     to move on. In addition, Taylorism, time-and-motion studies, and related approaches to
     "scientific management" in wide use at the time tended to view workers as machines,
     and new (younger) machines worked better than old machines. See Dora L. Costa,
     History of Retirement, op.cit., pp. 23-25.

82   In the US, the Civil War veterans' pension, established by Congress in 1862, was our first
     experience with a government pension. In 1902, payments to nearly one million Civil
     War pensioners amounted to nearly 30 percent of the federal budget. Government
     pensions then spread among the states, culminating in 1935, with a federal, universal
     old-age pension we call Social Security. The railroads were among the first to provide
     private pensions. However, today even private pensions are, with limits, guaranteed by
     the government through the federal Pension Benefit Guarantee Corporation (PBGC).
     See Dora L. Costa, History of Retirement, op.cit., p. 198.

83   For a brief but excellent history of Social Security, including attention to political, social
     and economic forces that shaped it, see the Social Security Administration's 30-page
     Historical Background and Development of Social Security, found online at http://www.
     socialsecurity.gov/history/briefhistory3.html.

84   Del Webb invented what we now call the retirement community. The first was called
     Sun City. It opened on January 1, 1960, in what is now the metropolitan area of Phoenix,
     Arizona. Sun City reflected Webb's novel concept of an age-restricted (e.g., 55 years or

more), lifestyle community where "active adults" can pursue old passions and hobbies, discover new interests, and engage with like-minded people. Today, there are more than 50 Del Webb communities across 20 states. Age-restricted retirement communities are now commonplace in the US and in many other parts of the world.

85   The study, conducted by Nyhart, an actuarial and employee benefits consulting firm, is based on a review of nearly 10,000 401(k) and related retirement accounts from employees at 110 public and private companies. Results show that 81 percent of employees 18 or older will not be able to afford to retire by the age of 65. The study blames it on "their failure to contribute enough of their income towards retirement." See Joe Mont, "Retirement Study Calls 73 the New 65," The Street, December 6, 2010.

86   The Great Recession included a devastating stock market crash in 2008 – including an unprecedented decline in household net worth – from a high of $66 trillion before the Great Recession to a low of $49 trillion. By late 2010, household net worth had recovered to $55 trillion, but it was still $11 trillion below pre-recession highs. See Federal Reserve, Flow of Funds Accounts of the US, Third Quarter, 2010, AP report cited in The Capital (Annapolis), December 10, 2010, p. A7.

87   Retirees are still able to take retirement benefits at age 62, but payments will be reduced. See Social Security Administration table in Hinden, p. 39.

88   Though most of the chatter is about the solvency of Social Security, Medicare's unfunded liability is five times that of Social Security.

89   Unfortunately, my father, always a picture of health, passed away unexpectedly exactly two months to the day after arriving in Florida on January 2, 1982, to take up a new life. Though his passing was a sad and unexpected event, my parents managed their transition perfectly and finished well by any measure. My mother continues to live on Estero Island, sustained by many connections, some of which are rooted in vacations taken over many years, beginning more than 50 years ago.

7. Work Till You Drop

90   Mex Cooper, "Catholic Church tells Fr. Bob Mcguire to retire, The Age (Melbourne, Australia), September 7, 2009.

91   From J. Martin Klotsche and Adolph A. Suppan, Life Begins at Eighty, op. cit., p. 35.

92   For his work on vascular suture and the transplantation of blood vessels and organs, Carrel was awarded the 1912 Nobel Prize in Medicine. In collaboration with famed pilot Charles A. Lindbergh, he also co-authored The Culture of Organs, and worked with engineer Lindbergh in the mid-1930s to create the "perfusion pump," which allowed living organs to exist outside of the body during surgery, an advance that laid the foundation for open-heart surgery, organ transplants, and the artificial heart, which became a reality decades later. Cited in Marie Beynon Ray, The Best Years of Your Life, op. cit., p. 28.

93   Charles Handy, The Age of Unreason, Cambridge: Harvard Business School Press, 1989.

94   Oliver Wendell Holmes, Radio Address, in Sheldon M. Novick (ed.), the Collected Works of Justice Holmes, vol. 1, Chicago: University of Chicago Press, 1995, cited in Gilbert C. Meilaender (ed.), Working: Its Meaning and Limits, South Bend: Notre Dame University Press, 2000, p. 135.

95   Reference is to a University of Michigan study, cited in Mitch Anthony, The New Retirementality, op. cit., p. 79.

96   Stokowski (1882-1977), died with his boots on, one year later, at the age of 95. Stokowski led the Cincinnati Symphony at age 26, the Philadelphia Orchestra at age 30, served as co-conductor (with Arturo Toscanini) of the New York Philharmonic at age 67, and led the Houston Symphony Orchestra at age 73. At age 83 he was named conductor of the London Symphony. Based on J. Martin Klotsche and Adolph A. Suppan, Life Begins at Eighty, p. 65; and http://en.wikipedia.org/wiki/Leopold_Stokowski

97   It is sometimes hard to believe, but America was a rural nation at the beginning of the 20th century when more than 40 percent of the labor force was engaged in some form of agriculture.

98   During my boyhood in Lafayette, Indiana, we shopped at a corner grocery store where the proprietor and his family (who also worked in the store) lived in the back rooms of the premises.

99   On the evolution of home-based businesses in the US, see Marilyn and Tom Ross, Country Bound: Trade Your Business Suit Blues for Blue Jean Dreams, Buena Vista, Colorado: Creativity Communications, 1992.

100 On the modern home-based business, see Paul and Sarah Edwards, Working from Home: Everything You Need to Know about Living and Working under the Same Roof, New York: Putnam, 2006.

101 See, for example, Dan Buettner, The Blue Zone, op. cit., and David Hackett Fisher, Growing Old in America, New York: Oxford University Press, 1977.

102 D. Michael Bennethum, Listen! God is Calling!: Luther Speaks of Vocation, Faith, and Work, Minneapolis: Augsburg Fortress, 2003. Bennethum is the senior pastor of the Reformation Evangelical Lutheran Church in Reading, Pennsylvania.

103 See Joanne Lynn, Sick to Death and Not Going to Take It Anymore!: Reforming Health Care for the Last Years of Life. Los Angeles: University of California Press & Milbank Books, 2004. See also June R. Lunney and Joanne Lynn, "Why We Know Painfully Little about Dying", Washington Post Commentary, March 27, 2005. Lynn works as a health policy analyst at the RAND Corporation in Washington, D.C.

104 Erik Erikson, Identity and the Life Cycle, New York: W.W. Norton, 1980 (1959).

105 "When people retire, they think they have lost their vocation." Cited in Robert Banks and R. Paul Stevens, The Complete Book of Everyday Christianity, Downers Grove: InterVarsity Press, 1997.

106   See John W. Rowe and Robert L Kahn, Successful Aging, op.cit.; George Vaillant, Aging
      Well, op.cit.; and Tony Buzan and Raymond Keene, The Age Heresy, op. cit.

107   Tim O'Reilly is a pseudonym. Tim agreed to my telling his story but not his real name.
      From an email of May 2, 2010.

8. Work-Life Integration

108   Mark R. Schwehn and Dorothy C. Bass, "Must My Job Be the Primary Source of My
      Identity?" in Mark R. Schwehn and Dorothy C. Bass (eds.), Leading Lives That Matter,
      Grand Rapids: Eerdmans, 2006, p. 186.

109   Marie Beynon Ray, The Best Years of Our Life, op. cit., p. 31. She also says on the same
      page, "Idleness is antipathetic to the nature of man...The proof of this is everywhere
      about us."

110   Cited in Helen Harkness, Don't Stop the Career Clock: Rejecting the Myths of Aging for
      a New Way to Work in the 21st Century, Palo Alto: Davis-Black Publishing, 1999, p.100.

111   George E. Vaillant, Aging Well, op. cit., p. 61.

112   See the Catechism of the Catholic Church, New York: Doubleday, 1995, Entry 2428,
      p.643. Italics added. This Catechism, the first new Catechism produced in 400 years,
      was mandated by Pope John Paul II and produced under the leadership of Cardinal
      Joseph Ratzinger, now Pope Benedict XVI.

113   This definition reflects several sources, including Bennethum, op. cit., and Webster's
      dictionary. Websters tells us that "work is an activity in which one exerts strength or
      faculties to do or perform something," including a: sustained physical or mental ef-
      fort to overcome obstacles and achieve an objective or result, b: the labor, task or
      duty that is one's accustomed means of livelihood, c: a specific task, duty, function or
      assignment that may be a part or phase of some larger activity." From: http://www.
      merriam-webster.com/netdict/work

114   Or, in the words of the Old Testament, "The Lord God took the man and put him in the
      Garden of Eden to work it and take care of it." Genesis 2:15.

115   John Piper, Don't Waste Your Life, Wheaton, Ill: Crossway Books, 2003, p. 139-40
      (Italics added).

116   On this point, see the work of David Miller and the Avodah Institute to "connect Sunday
      to Monday" and to "help leaders integrate the claims of their faith with the demands of
      their work" in business, commerce, and the professions. See www.avodahinstitute.com/.

117   The entire verse says, "Work is love made visible/And if you can't work with love but
      only with distaste/It is better that you should leave your work/and sit at the gate of the
      temple and/take alms of the people who work with joy."

118   From a speech by the Rev. Dr. Martin Luther King Jr., speaking in Kingston, Jamaica,
      on June 20, 1965, and recited by Martin Luther King III at Michael Jackson's memo-
      rial service in Los Angeles on July 7, 2009. Italics added. King's views echoed those

expressed more than 20 years earlier by British novelist and Christian essayist Dorothy Sayers who said: "The Church's approach to an intelligent carpenter is usually confined to exhorting him not to be drunk and disorderly in his leisure hours, and to come to church on Sundays. What the Church should be telling him is this: that the very first demand that his religion makes upon him is that he should make good tables...Let the Church remember this: that *every maker and worker is called to serve God in his profession or trade* – not [just] outside it." Dorothy Sayers, "Why Work," cited in Mark R. Schwehn and Dorothy C. Bass (eds.), Leading Lives That Matter, op. cit., p. 195. Italics added.

119   As this view of work implies, some kinds of activities would not qualify as work, begin-ning with the bank robber, the hit man, and other illegal or immoral activities.

120   Comment by Harvard psychologist Daniel Gilbert from provocative research reported in his bestseller Stumbling on Happiness, New York: Vintage Books, 2007. See also David Hochman, "Mirth Master Daniel Gilbert on How to be Happy," Reader's Digest, February 2010, pp. 16-17.

121   Perhaps the most interesting discussion of mutual obligations is Max DePree, Leadership As an Art, New York: Dell Paperbacks, 1989, especially pp. 35-51. Max DePree was the highly effective chairman and CEO of the very successful Herman Miller (the innovative furniture company). He looked at the mutual obligations involved in work as covenantal (not contractual) relationships, not unlike that between God and Man or between the pitcher and the catcher in baseball.

122   A term borrowed from Charles Handy, The Age of Unreason, Cambridge: Harvard Business School Press, 1989, p. 184.

123   My concept of Samaritan work is inspired by what Marvin Olasky calls compassion. Compassion, as Olasky reminded us in his important book, The Tragedy of American Compassion, is not about the emotion of caring, sensitivity, sympathy, or other such feeling words, now typically used as synonyms. Instead, compassion is about doing. Olasky reminds us that compassion is, at its root, about "personal involvement with the needy, suffering with them, not just giving to them." It is, as the 1834 edition of Webster's dictionary said, suffering with another. Compassion, in other words, is about one person personally involved in helping to meet the needs of another person. See Marvin Olasky, The Tragedy of American Compassion, Wheaton, Ill.: Crossway Books, 1992.

124   My term "enrichment work" was stimulated by Charles Handy's concept of "study work". See Charles Handy, The Age of Unreason, op. cit., pp. 184-85.

125   See, for example, Nicole Bouchard Boles, How to be an Everyday Philanthropist: 330 ways to make a difference in your home, community and world – at no cost, op. cit.

126   Dorothy Sayers, "Why Work?" in Mark R. Schwehn and Dorothy C. Bass (eds.), Leading Lives That Matter:, op. cit., p. 192.

127 My term "enrichment work" was stimulated by Charles Handy's concept of "study work." See Charles Handy, The Age of Unreason, op. cit., pp. 184-85.

128 John W. Rowe and Robert L Kahn, Successful Aging, op.cit., p. 179.

129 Though health, wealth, physical fitness, and mental acuity are all involved in successful aging, the best predictor appears to be social engagement. See John W. Rowe and Robert L Kahn, Successful Aging, op.cit.; George Vaillant, Aging Well, op. cit.; and Tony Buzan and Raymond Keene, The Age Heresy, op. cit. See also Marie Beynon Ray, The Best Years of Your Life, op. cit.; and Daniel Gilbert, Stumbling on Happiness, op. cit.

130 Cited in Marie Beynon Ray, The Best Years of Your Life, p., 28.

131 Oliver Wendell Holmes, Radio Address, in Sheldon M. Novick (ed.), the Collected Works of Justice Holmes, vol. 1, Chicago: University of Chicago Press, 1995, cited in Gilbert C. Meilaender (ed.), Working: Its Meaning and Limits, South Bend: Notre Dame University Press, 2000, p. 135. Italics added.

9. Work and Later-Life Satisfaction

132 George Burns, one of America's great motion picture, television, concert and recording performers, worked well into his nineties. See J. Martin, Life Begins at Eighty, op. cit., p. 16.

133 Betty Friedan, Fountain of Age, New York: Simon and Schuster, 1993, p. 222.

134 The Conference Board reports that about half of all Americans today say they are satisfied with their jobs, down from nearly 60 percent in 1995. The decline in job satisfaction is widespread among workers of all ages and across all income brackets. But among the 50 percent who say they are content, only 14 percent say they are very satisfied. See "US Job Satisfaction Keeps Falling," a news release by The Conference Board, February 28, 2005.

135 I told the story of my desire, rooted in my boyhood experience with my father's work with patent attorneys, to live my life in the law in my keynote address for the annual Fuji Xerox Australian Law Awards. See Philip M. Burgess, "Good Stories Make Good Law," Keynote Address, Fuji Xerox Australian Law Awards for 2006, sponsored by Lawyers Weekly & Australian Corporate Lawyers Association, October 20, 2006.

136 William Charland, Career-Shifting, Holbrook, Mass.: Adams Publishing, 1993.

137 See Philip M. Burgess, "From Flak Catcher & Spin Meister to Advisor & S'plainer Man: The Changing Role of the Business Communicator," Keynote address for the International Association of Business Communicators and the IABC Asia Pacific Leadership Institute meeting in Melbourne, Australia, November 7-8, 2005.

138 Excerpt from interview of Rick Warren, author of The Purpose-Driven Life, (Grand Rapids: Zondervan, 2002) by Meet the Press host David Gregory on November 29, 2009. Italics added. With more than 30 million copies sold, The Purpose-Driven Life is one of the all-time best sellers.

139 On callings and vocations, see philosopher and social critic Os Guinness, The Call, op. cit. and his Entrepreneurs of Life: Faith and the Venture of Purposeful Living, Colorado Springs: NavPress, 2001. For an interesting collection of readings, see William C. Placher (ed.), Callings: Twenty Centuries of Christian Wisdom on Vocation, Grand Rapids: Eerdman's, 2005. For guidance on how to discover your calling, see the very useful discussion and exercises in Richard N. Bolles, What Color is Your Parachute? 2010: A Practical Manual for Job-Hunters and Career-Changers, Berkeley: Ten Speed Press, 2010, especially Chapter 11, pp. 155 ff and Appendix A, and his How to Find Your Mission in Life, Berkeley: Ten Speed Press, 2005.

140 In Annapolis, there is a guy named Bob Moore, a West Point graduate and Army veteran retired to a Navy town and to a second career running a home inspection service for 20 years. After retiring from the home inspection business, he took a course in basket weaving, producing fine, intricately woven rattan containers called Nantucket baskets. After learning how to do it, "he now spends four hours a day working on baskets in his basement workshop, teaches basket-making classes, and also golfs, sails, and skis." Moore does it because, as he says, "There's a sense of accomplishment" in completing a basket "that can fetch hundreds or even thousands of dollars..." Reported by Theresa Winslow, "Making a Case for Baskets," The Capital (Annapolis), August 7, 2003.

141 Well-known examples of this view can be found in Studs Terkel, Working: People Talk about What They Do All Day and How They Feel About What They Do, New York: Random House, 1974; William H. Whyte, The Organization Man, New York: Simon and Schuster, 1956; or Arthur Miller, Death of a Salesman, New York: Viking Press, 1949. It is also noteworthy that job satisfaction is not necessarily related to income. A 2005 survey by The Conference Board shows that 55 percent of workers earning more than $50,000 are "satisfied" with their jobs, but only 14 percent claim they are "very satisfied." At the other end of the pay scale (workers earning less than $15,000), about 45 percent of workers are "satisfied," while 17 percent say they are "very satisfied." See "US Job Satisfaction Keeps Falling," a news release by The Conference Board, February 28, 2005.

142 As I recall, I was hired at $2.87 an hour, with a performance bonus on top, at a time when the minimum wage had just been increased from $.75 to $1.00 per hour. So even without the incentive bonus, I was making nearly four times the minimum wage.

143 Jim is a pseudonym because I can't recall his real name. It was a long time ago, the summer of 1956.

144 Working for Jim was tough. It meant you didn't take breaks and you didn't shut down for lunch. Instead you rotated through a lunch, taking eight to ten minutes (rather than the allotted 30) so that the press slowed down but never stopped producing.

145 Of course, if there is a calling, there must be a caller. In the Judeo-Christian tradition, that caller is God, and we are called to use our God-given gifts to carry out his plan for our life. See Os Guinness, Entrepreneurs of Life: Faith and the Venture of Purposeful Living, Colorado Springs: NavPress, 2001; Os Guinness, "How Do I Build a Successful

Life and Career?" in Joe Gibbs, Game Plan for Life: Your Personal Playbook for Success. Carol Stream, Ill: Tyndale, 2009. For the spiritual and the secular, answers may reflect familial, utilitarian, or even hybrid worldviews unique to the individual.

146   In his trial for heresy, when Socrates was charged with encouraging his students to think for themselves, to challenge the accepted beliefs of the time, and to work to make the world a better place, his defense was summed up in his statement, "The unexamined life is not worth living."

147   I don't recall Bob's surname. I met him once in a casual conversation at a swimming pool and remember him only by his first name.

148   Mark R. Schwehn and Dorothy C. Bass, "Must My Job Be the Primary Source of My Identity?" in Mark R. Schwehn and Dorothy C. Bass (eds.), Leading Lives That Matter, op. cit., p. 186.

10. The Two-Chapter Reboot

149   William Bridges, Managing Transitions, op. cit., pp. 3, 5.

150   Merton M. Sealts, Jr., The Journals and Miscellaneous Notebooks of Ralph Waldo Emerson, Vol. 5, Cambridge: Harvard University Press, 1965, p. 38.

151   William Bridges, Managing Transitions, op. cit., Chapter 6 calls this the "neutral zone."

152   The workplace can be almost anyplace in the digital age. If you are a knowledge worker, it may be at your computer in a conventional office, but it could also be on a telephone at home, at a summer getaway, on a boat, or in a hotel. See Philip M. Burgess, "From Gold Watches and Glass Towers to Nomads and War Rooms: How the Telecomputing Revolution is Shaping the New American Workplace," address for Understanding the Communications Revolution, a briefing for telecommunications trade media sponsored by Ameritech, in New York City, October 9, 1996.

153   The opportunity to perform is an important issue that needs to be addressed by public policy at the federal, state, and locals levels, and by corporate policy, and the elder care industry.

154   Based on data presented by David DeLong, Buddy, Can You Spare a Job? Westport, Conn.: MetLife Mature Markets Institute, 2009, p. 14.

155   Thomas Curwen, "Edwin S. Shneidman dies at 91; pioneer in the field of suicide prevention," Los Angeles Times, May 18, 2009.

156   Edwin Shneidman, A Commonsense Book of Death: Reflections at Ninety of a Lifelong Thanatologist. Lanham, MD: Rowman & Littlefield Publishers, 2009, p. xv.

157   Ibid.

158   I interviewed Ed Fergus on March 5, 2010. I am telling his story here with permission.

159   The term comes from Jane Jelenko and Susan Marshall, Changing Lanes: Road Maps to

Midlife Renewal, New York: Random House, 2008, an interesting book that includes the stories of people, both the well-known and Main Street types, who renew their lives by changing careers in mid-life.

160	Ed Fergus, another of the Greatest Generation, has had an amazing life, some of which has been chronicled in a three-part series in The Island Sand Paper, the local weekly newspaper of Fort Myers Beach. In World War II, he was Master Sergeant Edgar F. Fergus. Fergus became a prisoner of war in 1943 when his B-24 was shot down over the Adriatic Seas. He spent time in captivity in Italy, followed by a long ride in a boxcar into Nazi Germany, where he was a "guest" in various POW camps, experienced a harrowing ride through the mine-ridden Baltic Sea in a coal barge, and survived a 500-mile forced march in the dead of winter before his final walk to freedom 20 months later. See Edgar Fergus, "WW II Prisoner of War, Part 3," The Island Sand Paper, September 11, 2009, pp. 1, 14-15.

161	Email dated May 2, 2010. Teresa's last name changed at her request.

162	John the pharmacist was also ordained as an Episcopal priest at age 50, the onset of later life. It is not unusual to find that those who are über active and engaged in early and mid-life don't change their stripes when they enter later life. Cited with permission from an interview on February 5, 2010.

163	As you slow down with advancing age, ADLs begin to consume more of each day's waking hours.

164	Some ADLs, of course, involve schedules, but these are schedules that you set (e.g., medical appointments) or schedules set by others that are optional for you (e.g., putting out the rubbish).

165	See John W. Rowe and Robert L Kahn, Successful Aging, op. cit.

11. A Second Chance for All Ages

166	David Corbett with Richard Higgins, Portfolio Life: The New Path to Work, Purpose, and Passion after 50, San Francisco: Jossey-Bass, 2007, p. 21.

167	Howard Hendricks is Chairman of the Center for Christian Leadership at Dallas Theological Seminary.

168	Cited in Kerry and Chris Shook, One Month to Live, Thirty Days to a No-Regrets Life, Colorado Springs: WaterBrook Press, 2009, p. 127.

169	There is a vast literature on American exceptionalism. It begins with Alexis de Tocqueville's Democracy in America (1833) and continues with scholars, public intellectuals, journalists, and others, including: Gabriel Almond, Daniel Bell, Ray Allen Billington, Daniel Boorstin, Henry Steele Commager, W E B DuBois, Erik Erikson, Richard Hofstadter, Max Lerner, Seymour Lipset, Reinhold Niebuhr, Vance Packard, David Riesman, Arthur Schlesinger, and William H. Whyte. For a different take, namely that America is more like than unlike other nations, see Thomas Bender, A Nation Among Nations: America's Place in World History. New York: Hill & Wang, 2006.

170   The "Turner thesis" was famously advanced by University of Wisconsin history
      professor Frederick Jackson Turner in a paper delivered to the American Historical
      Association at the Chicago World's Fair in 1893, where Turner concluded that the
      sources of American exceptionalism were rooted in the movement of people to the
      frontier, a process marked by "breaking the bond of custom, offering new experiences,
      [and] calling out new institutions and activities." See Frederick Jackson Turner, The
      Frontier in American History, New York: Holt, 1921, which includes "The Significance of
      the Frontier in American History," his address to the American Historical Association in
      Chicago in 1893.

171   Generations earlier, in 1835, Alexis de Tocqueville made similar observations about the
      important role of unique, locally-based, voluntary associations created by ordinary
      American citizens in getting things done in the new nation called America. See Alexis
      de Tocqueville, Democracy in America, New York: Signet Classics, 2001, originally pub-
      lished in two volumes in 1835 and 1840.

172   Examples: citizen-based governance, e.g., the locally elected school board; experi-
      mentalism, e.g., diversity that comes with state control of curriculum; decentralized
      flexibility, e.g., policy-making and administrative control lodged primarily in state and
      local authorities.

173   The most accessible comparative data on spending for education, training, and de-
      velopment by units and agencies of government at every level can be found in the
      research and publications of the American Society for Training and Development
      (ASTD).

174   There are many respected proprietary post-secondary institutions in the US, such
      as the University of Phoenix, DeVry University, Kaplan, Capella University, and Gibbs
      College, to name a few.

175   Unfortunately, many so-called reformers in America are seeking changes that would
      further centralize, bureaucratize, and professionalize our educational system with a
      national curriculum and standardized national tests and other so-called reforms that
      would have many undesirable effects, one of which would be to slot kids early and
      greatly reduce the opportunity for the second chance. Most of these reforms, unfortu-
      nately, do not address the real issues that would provide reform in the direction of im-
      proved performance. See, for example, Neal McCluskey, "Behind the Curtain: Assessing
      the Case for National Curriculum Standards," Policy Analysis, #661 by the Cato Institute,
      February 17, 2010, a study that clearly shows that the "route to successful education
      goes in the opposite direction of national standards" and other conventional education
      reforms now popular in Washington; see also Evan Thomas and Pat Wingert, "Why we
      can't get rid of failing teachers," Newsweek, March 15, 2010, pp. 24-33.

12. Later Life and the Second Chance

176   Cited in Robert L. Dilenschneider, 50 Plus: Critical Career Decisions for the Rest of Your
      Life, New York: Citadel Press, 2002.

177 This view of life as a fleeting moment in time is expressed both in modern psychology (e.g., Rose Dubrof, "The Search for Meaning in the Later Years," in Robert S. Weiss and Scott A. Bass, "Challenges of the Third Age: Meaning and Purpose in Later Life, New York: Oxford University Press, 2002, pp. 173-187) and in the ancient scriptures, e.g., Psalm 90:12 in the Old Testament and James 4:14 in the New Testament. The quoted phrase is from James.

178 Kerry and Chris Shook, One Month to Live, op. cit.

179 From Facebook to the AARP online (see www.aarp.org/online_community/) many online communities cater to later-life groups around all sorts of topics, from dogs and stamps to singles travel.

180 Martin Gilbert, Churchill: A Life, New York: Holt, 1992.

181 Genesis 1:28 (NIV).

182 According to the "Religious Landscape Study" of the Pew Forum on Religion & Public Life (May-August 2007), 92 percent of Americans believe in God or a universal spirit, and 74 percent believe in life after death. On the other hand, we all know people who do not believe in an afterlife. For a rich discussion of the meaning of death by one who does not believe in an afterlife, see Edwin Shneidman, A Commonsense Book of Death, op. cit., especially p. 84.

183 Attention to the afterlife is seen most dramatically in the tsunami of articles and books about "near death experiences," so many, in fact, that "going to the other side" now has an acronym: NDE. For a particularly interesting example, see Howard Storm, My Descent into Death: A Second Chance at Life, New York: Random House, 2005. It is also noteworthy that many of those writing about these experiences were atheists or agnostics at the time of their experience. Of the many books about heaven, most of which, in my view, are quite dodgy see, for example, Roberts Liardon, We Saw Heaven: True Stories of What Awaits You on the Other Side, Shippensburg, Penn.: Destiny Image Publishers, 2000.

184 For example, read James 2:14-26 in the New Testament on why faith without deeds is no faith at all.

185 On the concept of worldview, see David K. Naugle, Worldview: The History of a Concept. Grand Rapids: Wm. B. Eerdmans, 2002; or Ronald H. Nash, Worldviews in Conflict: Choosing Christianity in a World of Ideas. Grand Rapids: Zondervan Publishing, 1992, where he details the four-chapter "creation, fall, redemption, restoration" worldview that dominates western story-telling, even secular story-telling and filmmaking. For a secular application of the worldview concept, see the work of Megatrends author and futurist John Naisbitt, Mindset, New York: Collins, 2006.

186 Despite all the real and substantial differences among the world's major religions, the Golden Rule is found in the Christian Bible, the Jewish Talmud, and the Book of Mormon, and in the sacred texts of Confucianism and Hinduism. See Stephen Prothero, God is Not One, op. cit., p. 2.

187   From Luke 6:31 (NIV) and throughout the New Testament, e.g., Matthew 7:12; Mark 12:33; Romans 13:9; and Galatians 5:14; and in the Old Testament, Leviticus, 19:18.

188   Matthew 22:39 (NIV). Though for Christians, Jesus raised the bar on this commandment when he said to his disciples the night before his death, "As I have loved you, so must you love one another." (John 13:34), and repeated it twice: John 15:12 and 15:17. On this point, see Dave Greber, The Lost Commandment, Grand Rapids: Kregel, 2009.

189   See David Guttmann, Finding Meaning in Life, at Midlife and Beyond: Wisdom and Spirit from Logotherapy. New York: Praeger, 2008. Logotherapy, developed by psychologist Viktor Frankl, refers to a form of psychotherapy that is based on helping people to find a sense of meaning and purpose in their lives.

13. Leading a Life of Meaning

190   Viktor Frankl, The Will to Meaning: Foundations and Applications of Logotherapy, New York: Penguin Books, 1969, 1988, p. 160.

191   The Dhammapada refers to Buddhist scripture traditionally ascribed to the Buddha himself. It is one of the best-known texts from the Theravada canon. Dhammapada is a compound word where dhamma refers to the Buddha's doctrine, or an eternal truth, or righteousness, or all phenomena, and pada can mean path or verse. See http://en.wikipedia.org/wiki/Dhammapada.

192   Mark R. Schwehn and Dorothy C. Bass (eds.), Leading Lives That Matter, op. cit., p. 187.

193   Viktor Frankl, Man's Search for Meaning, New York: Simon and Schuster, 1984.

194   One of the critical points in Henri Nouwen's development came with the death of his mother in 1978. Her death brought Nouwen face to face with his own struggle with the ultimate. See Henri Nouwen Society, A Remarkable Life: The Henri Nouwen Story, September 27, 2003.

195   Rick Warren is the founding pastor of Saddleback Church in Lake Forest, California, and the author of the international best-seller, The Purpose-Driven Life. This quote is from his Foreword to Kerry and Chris Shook, One Month to Live, op. cit., p. ix.

196   From a 1908 letter from Sigmund Freud to his daughter, cited in John W. Rowe and Robert L Kahn, Successful Aging, p. 45.

197   Melvin A. Kimble (ed.), Viktor Frankl's Contribution to Spirituality and Aging, Binghamton, N.Y.: Haworth Press, 2000.

198   Viktor Frankl, Man's Search for Meaning, op. cit., p. 110. Elsewhere Frankl says, "...meaning is no longer a matter of thinking but rather a matter of believing." See Viktor Frankl, The Will to Meaning,op. cit., p. 145.

199   On this summary of Frankl's approach, see James W. Ellor, "Bridging Psychology and Theology When Counseling Older Adults," in Melvin A. Kimble (ed.), Viktor Frankl's Contribution to Spirituality and Aging, p. 93.

200 See Viktor Frankl, Man's Search for Meaning, op. cit., p. 133. See also Melvin A. Kimble (ed.), Viktor Frankl's Contribution to Spirituality and Aging, op. cit., p. 145 and Victor Frankl, The Doctor and the Soul, New York: Vintage Books, 1965, p. xii.

201 See Henri J.M. Nouwen, The Prodigal Son: A Story of Homecoming, New York: Doubleday, 1992, especially pp. 3-14 for an account of his experience with the painting – what he saw, what he experienced, and how it affected the rest of his life. See also Nouwen's Home Tonight, op. cit.

202 For an interesting account of achievement and suffering from a patient interview by Frankl, see Viktor Frankl, Will to Meaning, op. cit., pp. 120-23.

203 John Steinbeck, East of Eden, New York: Penguin Books, 1952, pp. 413-415.

204 Ibid., pp 414-15. Italics added.

205 Our seeking to be good doesn't mean we succeed. For example in Romans 7:14-20, Paul says we are "slaves to sin" no matter how hard we try. "I am...a slave to sin. I do not understand what I do. For what I want to do I do not do, but what I hate I do...I have the desire to do what is good, but I cannot carry it out. For what I do is not the good I want to do; no, the evil I do not want to do—this I keep on doing."

206 Dallas Willard, Hearing God: Developing a Conversational Relationship with God, Downers Grove, Illinois: InterVarsity Press, 1999.

207 Princeton Review, http://www.princetonreview.com/schools/business/BizBasics. aspx?iid=1041402;

See also The Acton MBA, http://www.actonmba.org/about/.

208 This is from the message Jeff Sandefer delivered in an address to an incoming MBA class at Acton. See podcast at The Acton MBA, http://www.actonmba.org/about/. I learned about the Acton MBA program from a close friend who went to work for Jeff Sandefer. The more I learned the more I became impressed with what they do to shape the skills, values, and perspectives of their students. My son decided to get his MBA at Acton. It has been an education for both of us.

209 It is interesting to note how this idea conforms to the 40 days of Lent, which gives practicing Christians an annual occasion to reflect and reorient their personal and community life, a second chance to more closely represent the life and ministry of Jesus in the world.

210 For the Christian, that means we should love God, first and foremost, and then love others as he loves us. See, for example, John 13:34-35.

211 Richard N. Bolles and John E. Nelson, What Color is Your Parachute for Retirement, Berkeley: Ten Speed Press, 2007, p. 128.

212 One way to stimulate your thinking about those choices is to work through the exercises in Kerry and Chris Shook's One Month to Live, op. cit., an outstanding book that

will focus your mind and stimulate your thinking. See also Viktor Frankl, Man's Search for Meaning, op. cit., and Romans 7:7-25 and Paul's discussion of the wages of sin.

213   See Henry T. Blackaby and Claude V. King, Experiencing God: Knowing and Doing the Word of God, Nashville: Broadman and Holman, 1994, and a workbook of study questions by the same name published in 1998.

214   See John Micklethwait and Adrian Wooldridge, God is Back, New York: Penguin Press, 2009, for an insightful account of how the global revival of faith is changing the world, in some ways for the good, and in others, not so good. See also Frank Luntz, "God Help Us", a chapter in his What Americans Really Want: The Truth About Our Hopes, Dreams, and Fears. New York: Hyperion, 2009, pp. 157-177.

215   I will never forget my first and only experience at a silent retreat. A close friend, a former Jesuit, invited me to join him for five days at a retreat house in Colorado. I accepted and discovered only after arriving that it was a silent retreat. I felt like I had been on the wrong end of a bait-and-switch by one of my best friends. I surely was not thrilled about a week of keeping my lips zipped. However by early in the second day, the hush of silence, the value of listening, and time to reflect really began to sink in. Those five days turned out to be five of the most important days in my spiritual development. I don't know if it's an urban legend or not, but I have since read someplace that the caution to remain silent – be slow to speak, hold your tongue, listen, etc. – is the most repeated admonition in the Bible after the admonition to "love God."

216   Found in the Old Testament (Leviticus 18:19) and the New Testament Gospels, for example, Matthew 22:36-40: "Teacher, which is the greatest commandment in the Law?" Jesus replied: "Love the Lord your God with all your heart and with all your soul and with all your mind.' This is the first and greatest commandment. And the second is like it: 'Love your neighbor as yourself.' All the Law and the Prophets hang on these two commandments." See also Mark 12:28-31.

217   The call to the Golden Rule or to serve others, to "love your neighbor as yourself" is found in both the Old Testament (e.g., Deuteronomy 6:4-6; Isaiah 58:6-11; Micah 6:7-8) and the New (e.g., Matthew 22:37-39; Matthew 25:34-40; Mark 12:31).

218   See, for example, man's stewardship responsibilities, outlined in Genesis 1:28: "God blessed them and said to them, 'Be fruitful and increase in number; fill the earth and subdue it. Rule over the fish of the sea and the birds of the air and over every living creature that moves on the ground.'" Also in Genesis 2:15: "The Lord God put the man in the Garden of Eden. He put him there to work its ground and to take care of it." Responsible stewardship is also the theme of the Parable of the Talents (Matthew 25:14-30; Luke 19:12-27) where the master praises his servants who invest their gifts to expand the wealth they were given – and is critical of the servant who simply returns his gift. Stewardship is also embedded in the Social Gospel perspective rooted in the late 19th and early 20th centuries of the US. The social gospel movement called Christians not only to address, but to participate in solving the social and political problems of the world. According to social gospel writer John Bower, "This action is not in the hope of

making the world a paradise. It is simply to help make it a more tolerable place, to help bring order where there is disorder...equity must emerge...slavery must be condemned. Oppression of the poor by the rich should be condemned..." See John Bower, "Social Action: A Christian Mandate," Direction Journal, January 1978, pp. 3-10. For a related view, see Francis Schaeffer, A Christian Manifesto, Wheaton, Ill: Crossway Books, 2005 (1981).

219 An apt phrase from Robert S. Weiss and Scott A. Bass, "Epilogue: Concluding Note on Meaning and the Possibility of Productive Aging," in their Challenges of the Third Age, op.cit, p. 193. Repairing the world (tikkun olam in the Hebrew) is key element of Hebrew tradition, where "redemption is this worldly, accomplished not in heaven but here on earth. And it comes by doing rather than believing...Whereas Christians strive to keep the faith, Jews strive to keep the commandments." See Stephen Prothero, God is Not One, op.cit. pp. 245. 252.

220 In the words of Os Guinness, "Our primary calling as followers of Christ is by him, to him and for him. First and foremost we all called to Someone (God), not to something (such as motherhood, politics, or teaching) or to somewhere (such as the inner city or Outer Mongolia)." See Os Guinness, Rising to the Call, op. cit.

221 One of the most popular and influential books of the Social Gospel movement is Charles M. Sheldon's In His Steps, Uhrichsville, Ohio: Barbour Books, 1993 – originally published in 1887 but still in print and widely read. According to Sheldon, American society would experience a dramatic transformation if people of faith would pledge for an entire year not to do anything personal or vocational lives without first asking themselves, "What Would Jesus Do?" The book tells the story of what happens to the newspaper man, the theater owner, and others in the community. In His Steps has sold more than 15 million copies and is still widely read by Christian evangelicals. In His Steps is also the source for the recently popular WWJD movement and the WWJD motto found on bracelets and pins, symbolizing the bearer's personal commitment to be a follower and not just a believer, to walk the talk, to conduct oneself according to the teachings of Jesus.

222 Leo Strauss, Natural Right and History, Chicago: University of Chicago Press, 1953, p. 15.

223 While nearly every one of the world's eight great religions affirms a divinity, it is important to note, as Stephen Prothero has said, that one is not the only number: "Many Buddhists believe in no god, and many Hindus believe in thousands. Moreover, the characters of these gods differ wildly. Is God a warrior like Hinduism's Kali or a mild-mannered wanderer like Christianity's Jesus? Is God personal, or impersonal? Male, or female (or both)? Or beyond description altogether?" See Stephen Prothero, God is Not One, op.cit. p. 2.

224 For the best one-stop portrait of the many facets of the religious beliefs and practices of the American people, see the continuing studies, including respected opinion research, of the Pew Center on Religion & Public Life. Over-all, Pew studies have shown that 92 percent of Americans believe in God or a universal spirit, and 74 percent believe in life after death. For state-by-state assessments that profile belief in God, frequency of

prayer, and attendance at worship services, see http://pewforum.org/How-Religious-Is-Your-State-.aspx. Another good source of data about and professional analysis of the religious beliefs and practices of Americans is The Barna Group in Ventura, California. See, for example, George Barna, The Seven Faith Tribes: Who They Are, What They Believe, and Why They Matter, Carol Stream, Illinois: Tyndale House, 2009.

225   For a novel and interesting discussion of the role of the secular in the context of Judeo-Christianity, see John Markus, Christianity and the Secular, Notre Dame, Indiana: University of Notre Dame Press, 2006. Markus makes a distinction between the secular person and the non-spiritual or "profane. The difference is the non-spiritual is anti-religion and actively rejects the transcendent. The secular is not a believer in the religious sense, but is not hostile to religion and often has a worldview that affirms a role for the transcendent in day-to-day life. Markus argues that Christianity, alone among the world religions, has a place for and is accepting of the secular person...i.e., the non-believer. The Greco-Roman religions and other world religions generally divide the world into the sacred and the profane. See Markus, Chapter 1, pp. 13 ff.

226   See, for example, Anthony Robbins, Unlimited Power: The New Science of Personal Achievement. New York: Simon & Schuster, 1986; Stephen Covey's best-seller, The Seven Habits of Highly Effective People, New York: The Free Press, 1989; Wayne W. Dyer, Real Magic: Creating Miracles in Everyday Life, New York: HarperCollins, 1992.

227   The Dale Carnegie program, initiated in 1912, is still active and has touched more than eight million people in 75 countries around the world. See Dale Carnegie, How to Win Friends and Influence People, New York: Simon and Shuster, 1937.

228   Dyer is often seen on PBS as a popular fund-raising season performer where he talks about how to achieve personal growth. See, for example, Wayne W. Dyer, Inspiration: Your Ultimate Calling, Carlsbad, California: Hay House, 2006.

229   See, for example, don Miguel Ruiz and don Jose Ruiz, The Fifth Agreement: A Practical Guide to Self-Mastery, San Rafael, California: Amber-Allen Publishing, 2009, an extension of don Miguel Ruiz's 1997 New York Times best-seller, The Four Agreements, which sold more than four million copies. The five agreements are (1) be impeccable with your word, (2) don't take anything personally, (3) don't make assumptions, (4) always do your best, (5) be skeptical, but learn to listen.

14. Time-Out to Script a New Life

230   Richard Bolles, author of the widely read What Color is Your Parachute, offers a practical way for Christians to think about their life's mission and a practical, job-related interpretation of scripture that will work for most people in the Judeo-Christian tradition. See Richard N. Bolles, What Color is Your Parachute: A Practical Manual for Job-Hunters and Career-Changers, Berkeley: Ten Speed Press, 2010, especially Appendix A: "Finding Your Mission in Life, pp. 245-263.

231   Leslie Milk is the lively lifestyle editor of the Washingtonian magazine. She said this to me at dinner one evening during a conversation about retirement as a disease.

232　From the poem "The Lost Years", penned by the young John Piper; cited in John Piper, Don't Waste Your Life, Wheaton, Ill: Crossway Books, 2003, p. 14.

233　For a discussion of the advantages of later life and the assets we bring to it, see Gene D. Cohen, The Creative Age: Awakening Human Potential in the Second Half of Life, New York: HarperCollins/Avon Books, 2001.

234　My views about transitions have been most influenced by the work of William Bridges. On the structure and process of transitions, see William Bridges, Transitions: Making Sense of Life's Changes. (Cambridge: Perseus Books, Da Capo Press, 2004). For a more practical approach for use at the level of the individual or the organization, see his Managing Transitions, op. cit.

235　The phrase, bucket list, comes from a Rob Reiner comedy, a film about redemption called The Bucket List.

15. Tools for a Time-Out

236　Mitch Albom, Tuesdays with Morrie: An Old Man, A Young Man, and Life's Greatest Lesson, New York: Doubleday, 1997, p. 18. Later on, when discussing Mitch's changing relationship with his own brother, Morrie tells Mitch, "There is no formula to relationships…You never want them to stop. But that's part of being human. Stop, renew, stop, renew." pp. 177-78. Italics added.

237　C.G. Jung, "The Stages of Life," in Joseph Campbell (ed.), The Portable Jung, New York: Viking, 1971, p. 12.

238　New Age author and a leader in the human potential movement. See her most influential book, The Aquarian Conspiracy: Personal and Social Transformation in Our Time, New York: J. P. Tarcher/Penguin, 1980.

239　David Guttmann,. Finding Meaning in Life, at Midlife and Beyond, op. cit., p. 13.

240　There are many good books on mentoring. Two I have found useful are David Kay and Roger Hinds, A Practical Guide to Mentoring: How to Help Others Achieve Their Goals, Oxford: HowToBooks, 2007, and John C. Maxwell, Mentoring, Nashville: Thomas Nelson, 2008.

241　See, for example, "Crafting Your Autobiography," on the Internet at http://homework-tips.about.com/od/paperassignments/a/autobiography_2.htm. The Australian movie, Ten Canoes – a lengthy parable about right and wrong that won a 2006 Cannes Film Festival award – has a wonderful scene where the elder Aborigine tells the younger Aborigine, who has been flirting with the elder's wife and who is restless with the long, drawn-out story of the elder, that "the best part of the story is in the telling." The same goes for the autobiography – the best part may be in the writing. See also "How to Write an Autobiography," a two-page outline available on the Internet at http://www.sarasota.k12.fl.us/bhs/bryan/bryan_auto.html.

242 For an insightful discussion of dominant themes in American culture, see Robert Reich, Tales of a New America, New York: Random House, 1988.

243 Bill Gates, Sr., Showing Up for a Life: Thoughts on the Gifts of a Lifetime, New York: Random House, 2009.

244 William F. Buckley, Jr., Airborne: A Sentimental Journey, New York: Scribner, 1976. Another event-based autobiographical account can be found in James D. Watson and Lawrence Bragg. The Double Helix : A Personal Account of the Discovery of the Structure of DNA. New York: New American Library, 1991

245 Henri J.M. Nouwen, The Prodigal Son, op. cit.

246 For a book-length autobiography of pre-mortem reflections about one's own death, see Edwin Shneidman, A Commonsense Book of Death, op. cit., p. xv, which the author calls "a disguised lengthy auto-obituary." For a guide to writing obituaries, see www.obituaryguide.com/; for an example of eulogies, a cousin of the obituary, see Imamu Amiri (ed.) Eulogies, New York: Marsilio Publishing, 1996.

247 Cited in Uncle John's Reader. Ashland, Oregon: BRI Press, 2009, p. 144.

248 Richard N. Bolles, op. cit., and Richard N. Bolles and John E. Nelson, What Color is Your Parachute for Retirement, op. cit., especially pp. viii-21. The retirement edition, after the first 21 pages, deals with health care, finances, where to live – i.e., issues covered by every other retirement books. Though the retirement edition is a good source for those who want to address the broader set of issues, so are many others.

249 See Eric Sundstrom, Randy Burnham, and Michael Burnham, My Next Phase: The Personality-Based Guide to Your Best Retirement, New York: Springboard Press, 2007; and Kevin and Kay Marie Brennfleck, Live Your Calling: A Practical Guide to Finding and Fulfilling Your Mission in Life, San Francisco: Jossey-Bass, 2005.

250 The VIA was developed by the VIA Institute on Character, a Cincinnati-based non-profit dedicated to advancing the scientific understanding of personality traits that are building blocks for the good life for individuals and society. See especially http://www.viacharacter.org/Practice/Exercises/tabid/132/Default.aspx, which covers some of the exercises.

251 See David Corbett with Richard Higgins, Portfolio Life, op.cit.

16. Time-Out To Be

252 Erich Fromm, To Have or to Be?, New York: Harper & Row, 1976.

253 Henri Nouwen, Home Tonight, op. cit., pp. 37 ff.

254 "Sharing in the suffering of others" is the true meaning of compassion. Compassion is about actions or doing, not about an emotion or simply "feeling the pain" of others. See Marvin Olasky, The Tragedy of American Compassion, Wheaton, Ill.: Crossway Books, 1992, and the discussion of "Samaritan work" in Chapter 8.

255 I found this approach to Be-Do-Have on an interesting wiki called Lategrowth: Continuing Development for Oldies. See http://lategrowth.wikidot.com/doing-having-being.

256 In addition to roles, there are virtues, as we seek to be grateful, involved, positive, humble, prudent, still, focused, disciplined, resolved, patient, frugal, just, etc. See Gordon B. Hinckley, Way to Be: Nine Ways to Be Happy and Make Something of Your Life, New York: Simon and Schuster, 2002, esp. pp. 10-11; Though written for teenagers and their parents, it is a wonderfully wise statement of virtues by the 15th president of the Church of Jesus Christ of Latter Day Saints (Mormons). See also William J. Bennett (ed.). The Children's Book of Virtues, New York: Simon and Schuster, 1995.

257 William A. Sadler, The Third Age: Six Principles for Growth and Renewal After Age Forty, Cambridge: Perseus Publishing, 2000.

17. A Compass for the Post-Career Years

258 Hammer (1898-1990) was an entrepreneur, oil man, art collector, and philanthropist who amassed his wealth as chairman and CEO of Occidental Petroleum Company. Cited in J. Martin Klotsche and Adolph A. Suppan, Life Begins at Eighty, op. cit., p. 27.

259 Cited in Ralph Warner, Get a Life: You Don't Need a Million to Retire, Berkeley: Nolo, 2004, p. 2.

260 Of course, for the Christian the moral compass would place "honor God" first on the list – honor God, help others, and improve the world.

261 Demographic trends are a challenge globally as well as in the US. See for example, Jack A. Goldstone, "The New Population Bomb: The Four Megatrends That Will Change the World," Foreign Affairs, January-February 2010, pp 31-43, where one of the four trends is the aging workforce in Europe, Canada, the US, and especially South Korea and Japan, among the developed nations, plus China – and how the increasing numbers of retirees and decreasing numbers of working age people could constrain the growth of economic prosperity (pp. 32-35).

262 See, for example, David Walker, Comeback America: Turning the Country Around and Restoring Fiscal Responsibility, New York: Random House, 2009; and C. Fred Bergsten (ed.), the Long-Term International Economic Position of the United States, Washington, D.C.: The Peter G. Peterson Institute for International Economics, 2009.

263 See Pamela Villarreal, "Social Security and Medicare Projections: 2009," Brief Analysis 662, National Center for Policy Analysis, June 11, 2009, p. 1. This number includes $89 trillion for Medicare alone. According to Villarreal, "Politicians and the media focus on Social Security's financial health, but Medicare's future liabilities are far more ominous... Medicare's total unfunded liability is more than five times larger than that of Social Security." The unfunded liability is the difference between the benefits promised to current and future retirees and what will be collected in dedicated taxes (such as payroll taxes) and Medicare premiums plus any earnings. According to Villarreal, "If no other reform is enacted, this funding gap can only be closed in future years by substantial tax increases, large benefit cuts or both."

18. Getting It Right

264 Morrie Schwartz, Letting Go: Morrie's Reflections on Living While Dying, New York: Walker and Company, 1996, p. 61.

265 The literature on women and aging is both interesting and varied. For a discussion that is particularly relevant to Reboot!, see Susan Nolen-Hoeksema, The Power of Women, New York: Holt/Times Books, 2010, especially Chapter 14, "Aging like a Woman," pp. 270-294. Dr. Nolen-Hoeksema, a Yale University psychology professor, cites research showing that "Women's lives get better instead of worse as they grow older... [Reflecting] their relational strengths, women enter older age with a strong network of close relationships with people they trust and who want to reciprocate their empathy, patience, listening, and care...Women's strengths help them to not only be happier in old age but to live longer and more healthy lives" (pp. 271-72). See also Lillian S. Hawthorne, Finishing Touches: An Insightful Look into the Mirror of Aging, Forest Knolls, Calif.: Elder Books, 1998; Nan Bauer-Maglin and Alice Radosh (eds.), Women Confronting Retirement: A Nontraditional Guide, New Brunswick: Rutgers University Press, 2003; May Sarton, At Seventy, New York: W.W. Norton, 1984; Sandra Martz (ed.), When I Am an Old Woman, I Shall Wear Purple, Watsonville, Calif.: Papier-Mache Press, 1991; Nancy Alspaugh and Marilyn Kentz, Not Your Mother's Midlife: A Ten-Step Guide to Fearless Aging, Kansas City: Andrews McMeel Publishing, 2003; and Carleen Brice (ed.), Age Ain't Nothing But a Number: Black Women Explore Midlife, Boston: Beacon Press, 2003.

Epilogue

266 Cited in John W. Rowe and Robert L Kahn, Successful Aging, op. cit., p. 177.

267 Nicholas Rollins, et. al., Spanish Dictionary, New York: Oxford University Press, 2009).

268 The Spanish word siesta refers to midday rest and is from the Latin, hora sexta, or the sixth hour. Counting from dawn, six hours is noon; hence midday rest. The siesta, a common tradition in many countries, especially warm weather countries, is the traditional daytime nap of Spain, and through Spanish influence, of many Latin American countries.

269 Webb Chiles, "Nowhere in particular," Cruising World, October 2009, p. 81.

270 Ibid.

271 See Kathleen Shaputis, The Crowded Nest Syndrome: Surviving the Return of Adult Children. Olympia, Wash.: Clutter Fairy Publishing, 2004.

272 A useful and now widely used term coined by aging guru Ken Dychtwald, a pioneer in getting us to think about the impact of aging boomers on American culture. See Ken Dychtwald and Joe Fowler, The Age Wave,op. cit.

273 Richard Croker, The Boomer Century 1946-2046: How America's Most Influential Generation Changed Everything, New York: Springboard Press, 2007. Croker observes

(p. xv) that "...boomers have been glamorized and reviled, applauded for their idealism and attacked for their materialism, praised for their innovation and condemned for their rebelliousness. Whichever of those characterizations may be correct, these 78 million Americans have changed the world – are changing the world – and they will come to do so for another 20, 30, or 40 years to come."

274 Former President Clinton used the phrase, "go out serving."

275 Philip M. Burgess, "Lone Eagles Nest in the West," Rocky Mountain News, September 15, 1992.

276 See Peter F. Drucker, Landmarks of Tomorrow: A Report on the Post-Modern World, Edison, New Jersey: Transaction Publishers, 1959, 1996; Management Challenges of the 21st Century. New York: Harper Business, 1999; and Management: Tasks, Responsibilities, Practices. Harper & Row, New York. 1973. See also Don Tapscott and Anthony D. Williams, Wikinomics, New York: Penguin Group, 2006.

277 St. Augustine, City of God, Book XIX, chapter 19, p. 880, excerpt from Gilbert C. Meilaender (ed.), Working: Its Meaning and Limits, South Bend: Notre Dame University Press, 2000, p. 132.

278 From Dora L. Costa, History of Retirement, op. cit., p. 134.

279 From Joanne Lynn, Sick to Death and Not Going to Take It Anymore!, op. cit.

280 Philip M. Burgess, "Lone Eagles Nest in the West," op. cit.

281 From Dora L. Costa, History of Retirement, op. cit., p. 134.

282 See, for example, the new Catechism of the Roman Catholic Church, the first in more than 400 years.

283 On the point about code of conduct versus philosophy of life, see Robert A. Markus. Christianity and the Secular. Notre Dame, Indiana: University of Notre Dame Press, 2006, pp. 19-22, a book reflecting his contribution to the Pope John XXIII Lecture Series in Theology and Culture.

284 Cited in Huston Smith, The World's Religions, New York: HarperOne, 1991, p. 319.

285 Dora L. Costa, History of Retirement, op. cit.

286 Informed by C.J. Fahey, "Religion and spirituality: Key elements of health promotion among older adults." Perspectives in Health Promotion and Aging, 9 (3), 1-8, Cited in Tanya Fusco Johnson, Handbook on Ethical Issues in Aging, op. cit., p. 80.

287 Referenced by Olympian and Australian swimming icon Ian Thorpe in a speech given at the "Beyond Sport Summit" in London on Thursday July 9, 2009.

288 John W. Rowe and Robert L Kahn, Successful Aging, op.cit., pp. 39-40.

289 William Bridges, Managing Transitions, op. cit., pp. 3-4.

290 Some earlier books took a positive view of aging, but they are not, for the most part, research based. For a good example of this genre, see

291 George Vaillant, Aging Well, op. cit. , especially pp. 203-11.

Sidebar Endnotes

292 From Colin A. Depp and Dilip V. Jeste, "Definitions and Predictors of Successful Aging: A Comprehensive Review of Larger Quantitative Studies," American Journal of Geriatric Psychiatry, vol. 14, 2006, pp 6-20.

293 Refers to our "capacity to turn lemons into lemonade and not to turn molehills into mountains." George Vaillant, Aging Well, op.cit., p. 206.

294 Source: http://www.avolites.org.uk/jokes/aging.htm.

295 Kelly Haverstick and Natalia A. Zhivan, "Older Americans on the Go: How Often, Where, and Why?," Center for Retirement Research at Boston College, (Number 9-18), September 2009; and Brad Edmondson, "Six Unwritten Laws of Western Migration," paper presented at a Center for the New West Forum, Where Have All the Californians Gone?, July 7, 1999.

296 Circulated on the Internet. Author unknown.

297 From Russell Muirhead, Just Work, Cambridge: Harvard University Press, 2004, cited in Mark R. Schwehn and Dorothy C. Bass (eds.), Leading Lives That Matter, op. cit., p. 190.

298 From A.E. Clark, et. al., "Lags and Leads in Life Satisfaction: A Test of the Baseline Hypothesis," The Economic Journal, vol. 118, pp. 222-243, cited in Tom Rath and Jim Harter, Wellbeing: The Five Essential Elements, op. cit., p. 118.

299 Tom Rath and Jim Harter, Wellbeing: The Five Essential Elements, Ibid., pp. 16-17.

300 Marie Beynon Ray, The Best Years of Your Life, op. cit.

301 "The 20th Century's Ten Great Public Health Achievements in the US," in http://www. whatispublichealth.org/impact/achievements.html.

302 This summary is based on a thorough and very interesting discussion of the cost of leisure in Dora L. Costa, History of Retirement, op. cit., pp. 148-55. For an excellent overview based on on-going studies of the impact of electronic and digital media on people of all ages, examine the work of Jeff Cole and the Center for the Digital Future at the Annenberg School for Communications in Los Angeles. See http://www. digitalcenter.org/.

303 Jackson Putnam, Old Age Politics in California: From Richardson to Reagan, Stanford, California: Stanford University Press, 1970, p. 53; quoted in Dora L. Costa, History of Retirement, op. cit., p. 168; and Edwin Amenta. When Movements Matter: The Townsend Plan and the Rise of Social Security. Princeton: Princeton University Press, 2006.

304 Based on "Grandma Moses Is Dead at 101; Primitive Artist 'Just Wore Out'", New York Times, December 14, 1961, and J. Martin Klotsche and Adolph A. Suppan, Life Begins at Eighty, op. cit., pp. 52-53.

305 Bennethum, op. cit., p.25. See also Roger B. Hill, History of the Work Ethic, 1992, 1996 at www.coe.uga.edu/~rhill/workethic/hist.htm. See also, Seymour Martin Lipset, "The Work Ethic – Then and Now," Public Interest, Winter 1990, pp. 61-69.

306 Gilbert Meilaender, "Friendship: A Study in Theological Ethics," Notre Dame: University of Notre Dame Press, 1981, pp. 86-103, and noted in Mark R. Schwehn and Dorothy C. Bass (eds.), Leading Lives That Matter, op. cit., p. 229.

307 Compare, for example, 2 Thessalonians 3:6-13 with the Parable of the Rich Fool, Luke 12:16-21. See Os Guinness, Rising to the Call, op. cit., pp. 26-29.

308 Based on Eusebius' Demonstration of the Gospel (312 AD), cited in Os Guinness, Rising to the Call, op. cit., pp. 26-27.

309 Today, however, there are many forces in the Catholic Church that lean toward the integrated view of work and the idea that all work is holy work. See José Luis Maestre, The Sanctification of Work, New York: Scepter Publishers, 2003. Maestre presents a theology of work by examining what it means to pursue God in ordinary life, focusing on (1) work and holiness, (2) evaluating work, and (3) lay spirituality.

310 See Luther's The Babylonian Captivity of the Church (1520). Cited in Os Guinness, Rising to the Call, op. cit., p. 28. Schwehn and Bass observe that "...Martin Luther, the first of the Reformers to formulate a racially new understanding of the Christian idea of vocation, argued that any kind of regular and legitimate work in the world – manual labor, parenting, and civic activity – could be a vocation or a calling so long as the Christian did that work out of love for God in service to mankind." See Mark R. Schwehn and Dorothy C. Bass (eds.), Leading Lives That Matter, op. cit., p. 45.

311 For Biblical sources of Luther's philosophy, see Genesis 1:28 and 2:15 in the Old Testament. The New Testament also encourages people to be industrious. See 2 Thessalonians 3:6-13; 1 Timothy 5:13; Luke 12:16-21.

312 See for example, Max Weber, The Protestant Ethic and the Spirit of Capitalism, New York: Allen and Unwin, 1930, and still in print and widely read.

313 From a speech by the Rev. Dr. Martin Luther King Jr., speaking in Kingston, Jamaica on June 20, 1965, and recited by Martin Luther King III at Michael Jackson's memorial service in Los Angeles on July 7, 2009. Italics added.

314 Dorothy Sayers, "Why Work", cited in Mark R. Schwehn and Dorothy C. Bass (eds.), Leading Lives That Matter, op. cit., p. 195. Italics added.

315 Dorothy Sayers, "Why Work?" in Creed or Chaos, London: Methuen & Co, 1947, pp. 47-64, cited in Mark R. Schwehn and Dorothy C. Bass (eds.), Leading Lives That Matter: What We Should Do and Who We Should Be, op. cit., p. 192-93. Sayers lived from 1893-1957.

316 J. Martin Klotsche and Adolph A. Suppan, Life Begins at Eighty, op. cit., pp. 67-68.

317   Kirk Johnson, "Seeing Old Age as a Never-Ending Adventure," The New York Times, January 8, 2010. On the other hand, USA Today founder and columnist Al Neuharth argues that people must "know when to lead and know when to leave" – referring to his call for Rupert Murdoch (80), Warren Buffett (80), and John McCain (74) to hang up their spurs. See Al Neuharth, "Age 80 Really Like Yesterday's 60s?," USA Today, March 11, 2011.

318   Tony Buzan and Raymond Keene, The Age Heresy, op. cit., p. 18.

319   Though I remember this event as I watched the Mexico Olympics as a young man, I first heard this story in the context of finishing well in a lecture by Dr. Howard Hendricks, at a Denver Seminary workshop on mentoring in 1997. This story is also found in a sermon entitled "Finishing Well" by the Rev. Rachel Hamburger, First Presbyterian Church, Burlingame, California (March 30, 2003), found at http://www.burlpres.org/rhamburger_03_30_03.html. Akhwari's heroic finish can be seen on YouTube at http://www.youtube.com/watch?v=Hq3rOMnLGBk. It is inspiring to watch.

320   From Mark Goulston, M.D., "A Good Man, A Good Death," The Huffington Post, May 16, 2009. Shneidman was also the founder of the AAS and the journal.

321   From Wikipedia, http://en.wikipedia.org/wiki/The_Bucket_List.

322   There are many interesting bucket lists on the Internet. For example, see Josh Lew, "50 Things to Do before You Die," Traveler's Notebook, July 7, 2008. Found at

      http://thetravelersnotebook.com/activity-guide/50-things-to-do-before-you-die/.

323   Based on Philip M. Burgess, "Stories Refuel Family Culture," Rocky Mountain News, November 25, 1997.

324   David Corbett with Richard Higgins, Portfolio Life, op. cit., p. 44.

325   Ibid., pp. 4-5, 12, and 47.

326   Ibid., pp. 44, 136.

327   New Directions, Inc. is located at 66 Long Wharf, Boston, MA 02110-3620 and can be reached by email at info@newdirections.com.

328   Details about the AARP awards can be found at www.AARP.org.

329   See the research and publications of the Center for Work-Life Policy at www.worklife-policy.org.

INDEX

*Note: Pages followed by a "f" indicate a figure;
pages followed by a "s" indicate a sidebar.*

B

CPSIA information can be obtained at www.ICGtesting.com
Printed in the USA
LVOW041608090212

267958LV00003B/2/P